D0975159

TEN
STUPID THINGS
THAT KEEP
CHURCHES
FROM GROWING

How Leaders Can Overcome Costly Mistakes

TEN STUPID THINGS THAT KEEP CHURCHES FROM GROWING

GEOFF SURRATT

ZONDERVAN®

ZONDERVAN.com/
AUTHORTRACKER
follow your favorite authors

ZONDERVAN

Ten Stupid Things That Keep Churches from Growing
Copyright © 2009 by Geoff Surratt

This title is also available as a Zondervan ebook.
Visit www.zondervan.com/ebooks.

This title is also available in a Zondervan audio edition.
Visit www.zondervan.fm.

Requests for information should be addressed to:

Zondervan, *Grand Rapids, Michigan 49530*

Library of Congress Cataloging-in-Publication Data

Surratt, Geoff, 1962-
    Ten stupid things that keep churches from growing : how leaders can overcome
costly mistakes / Geoff Surratt.
        p. cm.
    ISBN   978-0-310-28530-4 (hardcover, jacketed)
    1. Church growth. I. Title.
BV652.25.S87 2009
254'.5 — dc22   2008044721

Published in association with the literary agency of Mark Sweeney & Associates, Bonita
Springs, Florida 34135

Interior design by Christine Orejuela-Winkelman
Cartoons by Mark Sheeres (sheeresillustration.com)

Printed in the United States of America

09 10 11 12 13 14 • 24 23 22 21 20 19 18 17 16 15 14 13 12 11 10 9 8 7 6 5 4 3 2 1

CONTENTS

WHO ARE YOU
CALLING STUPID?

I have a confession to make: my name is Geoff and I am a church addict.

Church is in my genes. My mom played the church organ on the night I was born, and she was back on the organ bench the next Sunday morning. My grandfather was a pastor, my father was a pastor, my brothers are pastors, and my sister is married to a pastor. I won't go into all of the cousins, uncles, and assorted other relatives who pastor or have pastored somewhere in America. Let me just say if I don't have a relative already pastoring in your community, I'm sure one will be coming soon. My family would start our own cult, but we can't agree on who gets to be the leader. The point is that church is in my blood. I have worked for or pastored a church since I was twenty years old, and somewhere along the way I have committed every stupid mistake in this book.

As a church addict, I find that nothing is more exciting than seeing a church that is growing. I love growing churches, whether they are across the country, across the county, or across the street. I can't imagine anything more fulfilling than being involved in a ministry that is making a dent in the number of people who will eventually face an eternity without God. It doesn't matter if it's a seeker-sensitive church, a purpose-driven church, a traditional church, or an emerging church; I love growing churches. To paraphrase Willow Creek Community Church founder Bill Hybels, growing churches are the hope of the world.

And as a church addict, nothing is more frustrating than walking into a really good church with a really sharp pastor and discovering that the church isn't growing. The pastor is pouring his life into this body of believers, but in spite of his very best efforts and sincere prayers, the most he can hope for is to have as many people attending this year as last. He has a deep desire to send out missionaries from his congregation, to plant churches in other communities, to see his people growing to spiritual maturity on a daily basis. You can see in his eyes and hear in his voice that one of his greatest desires is to see his church grow, but week after week, month after month, very little happens.

Before we dive in, I need to clarify a few things. First of all, God is sovereign. God blesses whomever he wants to bless, and he doesn't need any input from me about how to accomplish this blessing. Church growth tips, strategy sessions, and paradigm shifts are meaningless outside of the divine providence of our heavenly Father. If God decides to bless your church, he can do it in spite of you, me, or anyone else. If he decides to withhold his blessing, no plan, program, or prescription will make a difference. The guidance in this book is not meant as a substitute for the supernatural blessing of God.

Second, numerical growth in a church does not always indicate God's blessing. Some churches grow without God's involvement, and other churches don't grow even though they are right in the middle of his will. Just because your church isn't growing numerically doesn't mean God is not at work.

Third, I'm going to assume some things about the pastors reading this book.* I'm going to assume that you are sold out to God body, mind, and spirit. I'm going to assume that you would cut off your right arm if that would lead more people into a growing relationship with Jesus Christ. I'm going to assume that the only reason you want your church to grow is to see people experience God in a way they will never experience without becoming a part of a vibrant community of believers. If those things aren't true, fixing all ten of these mistakes

* One thing I am not assuming is that all pastors are men. Although I have used male references throughout the book, these principles also apply to female pastors.

won't matter a hill of beans. The task of growing world-changing churches is for pastors with integrity, character, and a raging desire to charge hell with a water pistol.

My experience in meeting hundreds of pastors over the past three decades is that most of them fit this description. They sincerely want to reach lost people, see people fully devoted to Christ, and help people find their way back to God. They read lots of books, go to as many church conferences as they can, and shift paradigms like gears in a '74 Volkswagen, but many of them find that their churches never grow. (Except on Easter when most churches in America grow for about ninety minutes.) Occasionally churches don't grow because of an inherent flaw in theology or practice. For example, snake-handling churches, by the very nature of their membership requirements, may be limited in their outreach. A lot of churches, however, seem to be basically sound doctrinally, are located in a place that is accessible without the use of a compass and a guide dog, and have a pastor who can present a relatively coherent explanation of the gospel. And yet they don't grow. I think sometimes there is a simple explanation: the pastor may be doing something stupid.

I'm not saying the pastor is stupid (although I'm convinced that anyone who would willingly become a pastor must have either a divine call or an intelligence deficit). The challenge is seldom intelligence; the problem is often perspective. Many times we are so close to the action that we can't see our own mistakes and we end up making decisions that undermine the very outcome we desire. And we are often the last person to realize the futility of the decision. We are so fired up, so focused, so committed to the cause that we can't step back and see that we are our own worst enemy. We need someone from the outside, someone we can trust, someone not afraid to pop our balloon and point out the major flaw that is stunting the growth of our church. That's where I hope to come in: I want to be that friend who can bring fresh perspective.

One of my goals this past year has been to learn how to fish. Actually, I'd like to learn how to catch fish, as I have discovered that just fishing isn't all that interesting. One of the requirements of successful fishing in the tidal creeks around Charleston is that you have to be able to catch your own bait. (Growing up in Colorado, we caught our bait in the fishing aisle at Wal-Mart.) The only way to catch bait in South Carolina, however, is to learn to throw a cast net — a small round net with weights on the edges. I have read articles about how to throw a cast net, I have watched videos about how to throw a cast net, and I have stared intently at other fishermen trying to learn how they throw a cast net. (I've discovered this is not a good idea; fishermen don't like being stared at.) I have tried for a year to learn how to throw a cast net on my own, but I still don't have a clue. I've finally determined that if I ever hope to catch bait, and subsequently a real fish, in South Carolina, I am going to have to ask a friend with experience and a different perspective to point out the flaws in my approach to net casting. I am too close to the action to see my own stupidity.

Many pastors do not have a friend to point out the flaws in their approach to growing a church. Pastors normally hear from three categories of people. The first is their spouse. After a particularly rough patch of ministry, the pastor will say to his wife, "What am I doing wrong? Why won't our church grow?" In most cases, either his wife doesn't have a clue what, if anything, needs to be changed, or she knows what needs to be changed but doesn't want to put up with the emotional grief of pointing it out, or she is tired of the whole challenge of ministry and thinks what needs to be changed is her husband's career. While a pastor's spouse can give helpful insight, she will often keep her insider's knowledge to herself, choosing peace over growth. Harmony in the parsonage, however, doesn't always lead to positive change in the pulpit.

The second group pastors often listen to is their staff. These are people who owe their livelihoods to the competency and goodwill of the man leading the church. While they may see some flaws in the basic execution of ministry, they often prefer feeding their children to pointing out stupidity in God's anointed leader. Pastors hear comments from staff members like "Great sermon," "Good plan," and

"Nice tie," rather than "That's the dumbest idea I've ever heard." The pastor goes home believing he has the best staff on earth but continues to scratch his head over why the church won't grow. While in many cases staff members have the best perspective and greatest insight to share with the pastor, he may not be open to receiving their input. Again, we have harmony; we do not necessarily have a growing church.

When a church is struggling, the third group a pastor hears from is the parishioners. Sometimes, however, what he hears is flattery rather than fresh perspective. People are often looking for special attention to their needs, and they will use whatever means necessary to achieve their desired end. The young family wants the church to upgrade the nursery, the family with teenagers points out the need for a new youth pastor, and the older couple adamantly lobbies to sell the sound system and bring back hymn books. The challenge here is that well-meaning parishioners often have no idea what they are talking about. They have never pastored a church, they have a very limited understanding of what makes a growing church grow, and they often are thinking more about what's good for their own family than what might be good for the entire church. While the pastor may receive lots of feedback from the church members, he may find it tough to discern God's leading versus members' personal agendas.

Moses had this challenge when he pastored Sinai Desert Community Church. He knew he was in over his head, but he didn't have a clue what to do about it. He looked to his brother and sister for help, but they actually caused more problems than they solved. (Nepotism is rarely a good idea, but since I currently work for my brother, I left if off the list of stupid things pastors do. I like to eat.) Moses was so busy just trying to keep his head above water that he had no time left for his wife and children. He finally sent them to stay with his father-in-law. The work of the ministry was eating him alive, and he didn't know which way to turn. Eventually his father-in-law, Jethro, came to see how things were going in the desert. (And to bring back Moses' wife and children. My guess is that the grandkids were finally getting on Jethro's nerves, but I'm just speculating.) When Jethro arrived, he found a mess; Moses was running the nation entirely by himself. (We'll dig deeper into this issue in chapter 1.) While the solution seems obvious when we read Jethro's advice in Exodus, no one else had been able to give Moses the input he desperately needed. He needed a friend to look him in the eye and say, "Hey, Moe, stop being stupid." Jethro was willing to be that friend.

I want to be that friend as well — the one willing to point out the unzipped zipper, the broccoli between the teeth, the glaring mistake that others can't or won't bring to the struggling pastor's attention. Why, you may ask, am I qualified to point out other people's mistakes? Because, to paraphrase the apostle Paul, I am the chief of stupid pastors. Of the ten mistakes highlighted in this book, I have committed all of them. I have also had the unique experience of having many Jethros in my life to learn from. My role is not brilliant guru bringing down wisdom from the mountain, but rather experienced fellow traveler. When I point the "stupid finger" at you, three fingers are pointing back at me. (I'm not sure who the thumb is pointing at, but you get the idea.)

Let me give a little background on my experience as a stupid pastor before we dive into the ten mistakes. When I turned thirty in 1992, I had been on a church staff for ten years and I felt the overwhelming call to pastor a church of my own. I knew it was time to lead, to cast vision, to change the world. I considered starting a church but felt my gifts were more suited to leading an existing church to new heights. After exploring several options, I accepted the role of senior pastor (as well as children's pastor, youth pastor, church secretary, and janitor) of a congregation of fewer than twenty people (eleven to be exact) in a small town near Houston, Texas. During the brief time I was there, I did almost everything myself, I implemented every program I could copy, I clung to a terrible location, and I put the church ahead of my family; in other words, I piled stupid mistakes onto serious blunders. In spite of my blind spots, God did some amazing things while we were there. We saw amazing life transformation as people stepped from the kingdom of darkness into the kingdom of light and the church grew to about one hundred attendees, but we were never able to make the kind of impact I felt God had called us to. After two and a half years, the church had stopped growing, our finances were on the edge, and my relationship with my wife was strained. I felt like a failure as a husband, father, and pastor. I finally resigned as pastor and got a job teaching at a small private school. I didn't think I would ever work in vocational ministry again. Looking back, I realize what I really needed was someone to sit me down, look me in the eye, and say, "Geoff, don't take this the wrong way, but you are doing some really stupid stuff."

After two years away from vocational ministry, I accepted the invitation to join the staff of Seacoast Church in Charleston, South Carolina. Over the past ten years, I have had the privilege of being involved with a church that understands the value of asking tough questions and addressing glaring errors. Though we make more than our share of mistakes, God has blessed us with tremendous growth. When I came to Seacoast, we were averaging about one thousand people each weekend; currently we average more than ten thousand weekend attendees at multiple campuses located in three different states. During the past ten years, we have been able to send missionaries around the world, help plant dozens of churches across America, and transform several neighborhoods through community outreach. I have gathered a treasure trove of experience and wisdom from my years on staff at this amazing church.

The fact that I once pastored a wounded duck of a church and now serve on the staff of a megachurch, however, doesn't qualify me to call you or your pastor stupid. I get tired of people, whom God decides to bless for no apparent reason, suddenly becoming experts, writing books, and charging huge fees to tell everyone else how they should do things. So when I decided to write this book, I began asking for a little help from my friends. I knew that I needed to recruit some real experts if I wanted to discover some of the major stumbling blocks to church growth and ways to get past them.

Over the past few years, I've been able to connect with some incredible pastors from across the country. These are guys who have learned some tough lessons and are reaching a lot of people with the good news of the kingdom. Guys like Perry Noble at NewSpring in Anderson, South Carolina, who has more attendees at his church than there are people in his town (not literally, but close); Dave Ferguson at Community Christian Church in Naperville, Illinois, who has been able to plant more churches and opens more campuses in one year than most churches do in a hundred; and Mark Batterson at National Community Church, who didn't realize you can't build a church full of young singles in theaters in Washington, D.C., so he did. You'll meet the rest of the lineup as we go, but you get the idea. I could have done in-depth surveys, double blind tests, focus groups, and opinion polls, but since these guys know the answers, why not just ask them?

This book is not based on any one model or methodology. The insight is gleaned from pastors of megachurches, start-up churches, and many churches in between. The end result is an opportunity to learn from the experience of a wide variety of the best practitioners in the country — real pastors who are living the ups and downs of ministry on a daily basis. My goal is that this book will be a field guide for average pastors built on the experiences of other average pastors who are seeing amazing things accomplished in the kingdom.

Now let's dive into the first mistake and see if we can figure out what is keeping your church from growing.

TRYING TO DO IT ALL

"JUST BECAUSE I'M THE JANITOR
DOESN'T MEAN I CAN'T PERFORM YOUR WEDDING."

When I was pastoring little Church on the Lake in Texas, my schedule followed a similar pattern each week. I began every Monday morning by resigning as pastor. I told my wife and whoever else would listen that the church was full of whiners, the leaders were wimps, and the preaching was poor. Although they often agreed, by noon my little pity party was over and I headed into the office to start the week. The first task was to see if we were still in business. I checked the offering count from the weekend, saw what bills were due, checked our account balance, and breathed a sigh of relief if we had enough in the bank to pay the bills and my salary for one more week. I then found my way back to my office to begin praying that God would give me one more sermon. Actually, two more sermons, because I had to preach on Wednesday night as well. Actually, three more sermons until we finally canceled the Sunday night service after I decided I couldn't stand listening to myself speak three times a week anymore. (When I first started pastoring, I prepared four sermons a week because I also taught Sunday school. I quit teaching or going to Sunday school early on because I had always hated Sunday school as a child and figured I didn't have to go anymore now that I wore big-boy pants.)

Tuesday was accounting day. That was when I entered all of the tithe checks into the database I kept on my personal computer. I knew this wasn't the wisest way to keep the books, but it was better than the system they used when I came to the church. A sweet older lady we called Sister Dolly used to count the money, make the deposits, and write the checks. The challenge was that math wasn't Sister Dolly's strong suit. Occasionally she added checks to the balance rather than subtract them. That can cause some consternation at the end of the month. Once a month another volunteer took her work, mistakes and all, and transfered it into a handwritten ledger. Any expenses he didn't recognize he lumped into the miscellaneous category. One month we spent more on miscellaneous than on all the other categories combined. The next month I became the church bookkeeper.

On Wednesdays, in addition to coming up with a fresh word from

God for the handful of adults who would show up for Wednesday night Bible study, I began getting the music ready for the worship team on the weekend. When I first came to the church, we had two musicians: a piano player and a drummer. Listening to this little two-piece band was like hearing a train wreck in slow motion; we didn't worship as much as we held on for dear life and prayed that it would all end soon and on beat. Our deliverance came one Saturday afternoon a few weeks after I became the pastor. The piano player called to say that she wouldn't be there on Sunday so we would have to have "song service" without her. She wasn't good, but she was all we had. Without a lot of options, I rushed to our local Christian bookstore and found that they carried backup tracks to several popular worship songs on cassette tape. For the first time ever, our worship that weekend consisted of our worship leader singing along with a karaoke band. The congregation looked a little confused but relieved that for the first time the music wasn't painful; as bad as karaoke worship was, at least no one was injured in the process. The next week I told the piano player and the drummer that we were going to take a break from live music on Sundays and use backup tapes instead, and suddenly I became the worship director at our church. Every Wednesday for the next two years, I gathered all of our worship tapes and made a master tape for the weekend service. I then made duplicate tapes for the worship team, typed out lyric sheets, printed copies, and delivered everything to the singers. I was so focused on being the best pastor I could be that it never occurred to me that someone else in the church might be better suited for this job (considering I can't sing or play an instrument).

Thursday was sermon preparation and depression day. I spent part of the day working on a sermon for the weekend and part of the day feeling sorry for myself because I wasn't Bill Hybels. I had been to Willow Creek and knew that Bill wrote his sermons in a plush office looking out over Willow Creek's private pond full of seeker-sensitive ducks. (I imagined that's how his office looked; I'd never actually seen it.) I wrote my sermons in a converted singlewide trailer with burnt orange shag carpet, a window air conditioner that leaked, and geese that honked and left little presents on the front porch. Starbucks had not yet hit Huffman, Texas, so I did my sermon preparation alone and feeling sorry for myself. In my pity party I didn't realize that I could have pulled a team together to help write the weekend message with me. The congregation included some exceptionally creative and talented people who would have jumped at the chance to help shape the sermons; all I had to do was ask. But I didn't; I was the Lone Pastor.

Friday was bulletin and PowerPoint day. I typed up the bulletin, illustrated it with cheesy clipart, printed it, and folded it. Once my bulletin duties were done, I worked on the PowerPoint slides for worship and for my yet-to-be-completed sermon. If I had time once the bulletin and PowerPoint slides were finished, I hopped on the Sears garden tractor and mowed the grass for the weekend. Various repairs and maintenance jobs had to be kept up with as well, and occasionally I'd have lunch with a church member if there was time.

Saturdays were reserved for final message preparation and church cleaning. Every Saturday, I woke up with a knot in the pit of my stomach, knowing that in twenty-four hours I would stand in front of my congregation with nothing of value to say. This would be the week they would discover me to be the fraud that I was and would either laugh me off the platform or just stare coldly at me until I ran screaming from the building. By noon I usually had something that passed for a sermon and headed over to the church to clean. We had rotating teams of volunteers who came in to clean on Saturdays, but it seemed that every time someone got a sniffle, my family needed to step in and take their place. "Besides," I thought, "no one else cleans the church as well as I do."

Sunday school started at 9:30 a.m., and by 8:00 a.m. most Sundays Sister Dolly called to tell me who would not be able to teach class, work in the nursery, sing on the worship team, or fill some other essential spot at our little church that weekend. This early morning phone call always sent chills down my spine, but I usually detected a hint of glee in the voice of the bearer of bad news. My first instinct was to yell into the phone, "I don't care if Sister Mary fell off her porch and broke her ankle; she had better suck it up and get over to the church to teach our children about the love of Jesus." My second instinct was to explain to sweet little Sister Dolly that I didn't give a flip who taught Sunday school this weekend, laugh maniacally, and slam down the phone. Fortunately, I have seldom followed my first or second instincts in life, so each weekend, my stomach tied itself into knots as I thanked Sister Dolly for her thoughtful phone call and assured her that I would make sure the position was covered. Then I asked my wife if she wouldn't mind covering this weekend. If she was already doing two, three, or four other jobs (see chapter 2 on the wrong role for the pastor's family), I began calling everyone I could think of and begging them to fill in for just one Sunday. Usually by 9:25 most of the volunteer positions were filled by whomever I could guilt into exercising their spiritual gift of willingness to serve where coerced.

If you are scoring at home, I was the pastor, the bookkeeper, the Sunday school superintendent, the worship director, the administrative assistant, the groundskeeper, the maintenance man, the janitor, and the preacher. As I look back on my time at Church on the Lake, I can't help but wonder what I was thinking. We had capable and gifted people in the church who would have done a much better job than I did in most of these roles, but I seldom took the time to develop them or give them the freedom to make the job their own. As I've talked to pastors around the country, I've discovered I'm not alone. Trying to do all (or most) of the work themselves is the number one stupid thing pastors and leaders do that inhibits their church from growing. Inevitably in growing churches the senior pastor does less and less of the everyday work of the ministry, and the staff and volunteers do more and more. At Seacoast we have asked our senior pastor to cast vision, connect with leaders, and teach the congregation. He leaves almost everything else up to the leaders in the church. That is one of the major keys to the growth we have seen over the past ten years.

Why Pastors Try to Do It All

As we discussed in the introduction, pastors are relatively smart people, so why do they often try to do all of the work themselves? I think it comes down to several basic issues; let's address them one at a time.

Lonely Martyr Syndrome

Have you ever had this thought: "No one will do it as well as I will"? If you are like most pastors, you think no one cares more about the outcome of ministry than you. From designing the bulletin to picking up the trash to choosing the curriculum for the children's ministry, you are the only one who is really committed to excellence. You have given away tasks to others in the past, and they either did a poor job or dropped the ball altogether. You know you need to give away ministry to other leaders, but if you do, the quality of the ministry will suffer, needs will not be met, and people will leave the church. Rather than giving away ministry, you wind up taking on more and more tasks, stretching yourself beyond the breaking point.

If we were really honest, we would admit that deep inside we believe that the success of the church depends on us. And deeper down we would admit that we like it that way. We want to be in control. We crave the validation we get from praise. This attitude also feeds our bitterness and resentment toward people who we feel are using us. We adopt a martyr attitude and bear our cross for Jesus, relishing the role of the lonely martyr. Many of us cling tightly to the roles we have in our church because pride is rooted deeply inside our souls. Our church will not grow until we repent and turn to Jesus, rather than ministry, for fulfillment.

Hired Gun Disease

The thinking goes like this: "I am being paid to be the pastor. How can I ask volunteers to do my work for me? Besides, they have full-time jobs; they don't have time to do extra work around the church. We're taxing our people's time already by asking them to teach classes and attend small groups — we can't ask them to do even more. And what will the people think of me if I'm not working hard? They'll find out that other people are doing all the work and I'm lying down on the job."

My brother Greg, the senior pastor at Seacoast, has shared with me how he struggles with guilt in this area. At Seacoast he has built a teaching team of very talented communicators who share the load of weekend preaching. Everyone on the team loves the opportunity to teach, but Greg feels guilty asking us to teach. He feels like that is what he is paid to do and he shouldn't be asking us to do his work. We are each busy with our own assignments, and teaching just adds another burden. Over the past year we have helped him see that we love to teach and that being asked to teach on the weekend is a privilege, not a burden. One of the key factors in moving to a team-based ministry is getting past the guilt of giving away work and realizing that what is a burden for you is a blessing for someone else.

Corner Cutting Disorder

Sharing ministry is a lot of work; often it's easier to do everything myself. To share the load, I first have to identify what part of the ministry I will give away. Next, I have to find a leader who can take over the task. Then I need to recruit and train the new leader. This process can be difficult because I've never really thought through the steps of what I do; I just do it. New leaders, however, need a step-by-step process to follow. After I've trained new leaders, I need to coach them in their new tasks. When they make mistakes, I have to help them improve rather than stepping in and taking over. In the end, recruiting, training, and coaching usually take much more time and effort than doing the task myself. Many pastors work too hard and do too much because doing it themselves is simply easier.

Rejection Aversion

When I first saw Sherry Sparks, I knew I was in love. She was the foxiest-looking fifteen-year-old chick I'd ever seen. (That's how we talked in 1978.) The problem was that the thought of actually talking to her terrified me. What if she laughed at me? What if something fell out of my nose while I was talking to her? And most terrifying of all, what if I finally got the courage to ask her out and she rejected me? Fortunately, I was able to ask a friend to see if a girl he knew would ask her best friend to call Sherry and find out if she would be willing to allow me to call her. After thirty minutes of rehearsing my speech and several practice runs on the phone without actually dialing the number, I finally called the lovely Miss Sparks and invited her to our church's next youth group party. Two children and thirty-two years later, she still has that effect on me.

Sometimes we don't ask people to share the load of ministry because inside we are still that fifteen-year-old boy terrified of being rejected. What if I ask and they turn me down? Whether we're asking for a first date or asking a member to lead the prayer ministry, the fear of rejection is never easy to deal with. (By the way, it's a bad idea for a pastor to ask someone to lead a ministry while *on* a first date.)

Why Pastors Should Share the Load

One of the greatest leaders in the Bible is Moses. Here's a guy who took more than a million people for a forty-year stroll in the desert and somehow kept his sanity. Can you imagine how long it took just to stop for bathroom breaks? I know he was anger-challenged a couple of times when he beat the rock and threw the Ten Commandments, but overall Moses kept it together and did a very effective job of leading. He almost lost it early on, however. For the first few months of the journey, Moses looked like the Lone Pastor on steroids. He was settling every dispute, judging every criminal case, and hearing every lawsuit for a million people. The man was in serious need of a vacation. Finally, his father-in-law, Jethro, showed up right before they hauled old Moe off to the rubber pyramid. Moses told him about the escape from Egypt and invited Jethro to come to the office with him the next day.

> The next day Moses took his seat to serve as judge for the people, and they stood around him from morning till evening. When his father-in-law saw all that Moses was doing for the people, he said, "What is this you are doing for the people? Why do you alone sit as judge, while all these people stand around you from morning till evening?"
>
> Moses answered him, "Because the people come to me to seek God's will. Whenever they have a dispute, it is brought to me, and I decide between the parties and inform them of God's decrees and laws."
>
> Moses' father-in-law replied, "What you are doing is not good. You and these people who come to you will only wear yourselves out. The work is too heavy for you; you cannot handle it alone. Listen now to me and I will give you some advice, and may God be with you. You must be the people's representative before God and bring their disputes to him. Teach them the decrees and laws, and show them the way to live and the duties they are to perform. But select capable men from all the people — men who fear God, trustworthy men who hate dishonest gain — and appoint them as officials over thousands, hundreds, fifties and tens. Have them serve as judges for the people at all times, but have them bring every difficult case to you; the simple cases they can decide themselves. That will make your load lighter, because they will share it with you. If you do this and God so commands, you will be able to stand the strain, and all these people will go home satisfied."
>
> — Exodus 18:13 – 23

Jethro taught Moses several important lessons. First, he said, "What you are doing is not good. You and these people who come to you will only wear yourselves out." Moses wasn't just hurting himself;

the Israelites were tired as well. When we try to lead every ministry, we exasperate our people. It is much harder to get things done and to accomplish what God has called the people to do when everything has to run through you. Your people are getting tired.

The second lesson Jethro taught Moses is this: "The work is too heavy for you; you cannot handle it alone." No wonder Moses was at the end of his rope — he was trying to do the work of hundreds of people. When pastors are exhausted, their nerves are shot, and they want to quit every Monday, it's usually because they are doing their work and everyone else's as well. God has a huge vision for your church, but if you are trying to accomplish that vision alone, you will eventually damage your church, your health, and your family. One of the main reasons pastors burn out and leave the ministry is because they feel the need to lead almost everything. If it all depends on you, then we are all in trouble.

Jethro's third lesson is this: "You must be the people's representative before God and bring their disputes to him. Teach them the decrees and laws, and show them the way to live and the duties they are to perform." In other words, your job as a pastor is to preach the Word, model a godly lifestyle, and teach the people what they need to know to do the work of the ministry. That's it. That's your whole job description. Anything you are doing beyond that is wearing you out and getting in the way of others fulfilling God's call on their lives. The apostle Paul gives a very clear job description in Ephesians 4: "It was he who gave some to be apostles, some to be prophets, some to be evangelists, and some to be pastors and teachers, *to prepare God's people for works of service*, so that the body of Christ may be built up until we all reach unity in the faith and in the knowledge of the Son of God and become mature, attaining to the whole measure of the fullness of Christ" (Eph. 4:11 – 13, emphasis added).

What are we supposed to be doing? Preparing God's people for works of service. What are we actually doing most of the time? We're doing the works of service we are supposed to be preparing the people to do. So we wind up frustrated and exhausted, and we actually prevent the people from becoming mature followers of Christ. Oops.

How to Give Away Your Job in Four Simple (Not Easy) Steps

Step One: Connect the Dots

Your people want to be part of a big mission. Simply teaching a class, sweeping a floor, or printing a bulletin is not a big mission. People will grudgingly do these types of menial tasks until they can find a way out. On the other hand, when they can see these tasks connected to a bigger vision of changing their family, their community, and their world, they will arrange their lives around making sure the work is done. I saw this principle at work on a recent visit to Hillsong Church in London. When I arrived, dozens of friendly twenty-somethings were milling around the lobby wearing black "Ask Me" T-shirts. As I waited for the doors to open, I was greeted by charming volunteers offering platters of tea (very British) or coffee and informational brochures. As I talked with these volunteers, I discovered the secret to their committed service in what seemed to be menial tasks: vision. They each believed that through Hillsong they were part of a movement to change London and England and all of Europe. They weren't just serving tea; they were changing the world.

I found the same commitment in the volunteers at New Hope Diamond Head in Honolulu who arrive at 4:30 a.m. every Sunday just to cook breakfast for the volunteer staff. They consider it a privilege to serve the "Levites" who lead the music, teach the children, and do the other more traditional ministries. They are each committed to the vision, cast by Pastor Fernando Castillo, to change their part of Hawaii for Jesus. If you want to give away ministry to passionate volunteers, you must begin by casting a compelling vision.

Step Two: Make the Big Ask

Once you have cast a compelling vision, it's time to make the "big ask." Don't expect the right people to come forward on their own accord. Often the people who step up initially are the least qualified for the task. When I played football in eighth grade, our quarterback broke his collarbone during practice after our second game of the season. The first person to volunteer to take his place was Neil Owsley, our six-foot-two, 215-pound nose guard. Neil's role on our team was to make the other team's center cry, and he was very good at what he did. One team went through three centers in one game. Neil was an eager volunteer for the quarterback role, but he was not chosen.

Usually the best person to lead an area of ministry you want to give away is already too busy to volunteer. Effective leaders are seldom sitting around looking for something to do with their time. Your job is to find the right person for the job, share your vision for the ministry one-on-one, and then make the big ask. When Steve Jobs was recruiting the president of Pepsi to come work with him at Apple Computer, he is reported to have asked, "Do you want to sell sugar water the rest of your life, or do you want to change the world?" Jesus phrased his big ask this way: "Come, follow me, and I will make you fishers of men." The key to getting big leaders to lead big ministries is to ask them to do big jobs.

At Seacoast we call these big leaders high-capacity volunteers (HCVs). In HCVs we are looking for three things:

1. *A gift to lead others.* We need volunteers at every level, but an HCV is someone who is gifted to lead as well as serve.

2. *A higher than usual capacity.* HCVs don't need a daily task list. They need a problem to be solved and the freedom to solve that problem. A volunteer can be an usher; a volunteer leader can oversee a team of ushers; an HCV can rethink your whole approach to recruiting, training, and deploying ushers and implement that new approach.

3. *A heart and will to be used by God.* HCVs do not have to be coerced; they just need to be exposed to the right problem and given permission to discover and implement the solution. They want to be used by God; they just need a big enough challenge.

HCVs are completely changing our approach to ministry at Seacoast. We have former (and current) CEOs and CFOs of huge companies overseeing the business side of what we do. We have owners of companies teaching us about leadership and management in the corporate world and challenging us to translate the principles we learn to church. We have stay-at-home moms handling the administration of several ministries. Jesus did some pretty incredible work with high-capacity volunteers, and your church will be transformed as you make the big ask to your own HCVs.

Step Three: Show Them the Ropes

The biggest mistake we make as pastors in this area is that we don't hand off ministry; we abandon ship. Once we find a willing volunteer, we hand her the teacher's guide and the class roster and run like heck before she changes her mind. Imagine Jesus following his call to the disciples by giving them a three-page instructional guide on the principles of healing, exorcism, and new covenant theology and telling them to call if they run into any problems. Instead, Jesus devoted the next three years of his life to teaching, setting examples for, and correcting the disciples in the art of changing the course of history. The immediate effect of recruiting a new leader to take over a ministry area that you've been handling is that your life gets a lot more difficult as you show them how you have done the task, watch them as they do the task, and continue to give them feedback as they take over the task. When we fail to show new leaders the ropes, they either take the ministry in the wrong direction or don't last long in their new position. The long-range effect, however, of a strong mentor relationship is that the new leader accomplishes more through the ministry than we ever could have hoped or imagined.

Step Four: Quit

Don't quit the church; we have nine more stupid mistakes to talk about before we get to that point. But do realize that you are currently doing some tasks that you should pass on to someone else, while you are doing other tasks that nobody should be doing. Pastors who are overwhelmed by ministry often pastor churches with too much ministry. The most crucial step they need to take is to euthanize some part of their church. I know what you're thinking: "We can't stop doing Sunday night services or Wednesday night Bible study or Sunday morning adult Bible fellowship or Tuesday night prayer meeting or Saturday morning visitation; people would leave the church." In the words of Dr. Phil, how's that working out for you? Two excellent resources on finding tasks that you can quit altogether are *Choosing to Cheat* by Andy Stanley (Multnomah) and *Simple Church* by Thom S. Rainer and Eric Geiger (B&H).

It's Time to Clean Out the Garage

Every couple of years we go through a painful exercise at our house: we clean out the garage. Our garage has a defect in that it never stays clean for long. Whenever we get a new piece of furniture, we put the old furniture in the garage. Every time we get a lovely gift but don't know what to do with it, it goes in the garage. Every time my wife decides to change the decor of a room, all of the old decor goes in the garage. When the garage gets so full we can't open the door, we know it's time to clean it out again.

The challenge is that cleaning out always entails getting rid of stuff. All of the stuff in the garage has some kind of value, or we would have put it in the trash a long time ago. The problem is that if we don't get rid of some of the stuff, no matter how valuable it may be, we are going to wind up right where we started. So every time we clean the garage, we have to make difficult and ruthless decisions about what stays and what goes. Last time I lost my priceless collection of old broken computers. I still get a little teary just thinking about my first IBM XT rotting in a landfill.

Is it time for a garage sale in your ministry? You have been accumulating tasks and responsibilities for years, and it's time to give some stuff away and haul other stuff to the dump. What are you willing to pass on to someone else? What are you ready to see end altogether? Be ruthless — your church will never grow until you do.

For each of the ten stupid mistakes covered in this book, I asked the senior pastor of a growing congregation to give us his unique insight. Those interviews are included at the end of each chapter. Some of the answers are surprising, and though I don't always agree with everything they say, the perspective of these successful pastors is priceless. To get us started, I talked to Perry Noble from NewSpring Church in Anderson, South Carolina.

· · · · · · · · · · · · · · · · · ·**SPOTLIGHT**· · · · · · · · · · · · · · · · · ·

Perry Noble, NewSpring Church

My first impression when I saw Perry Noble was, "This is one big man." When Perry greeted me in his South Carolina drawl, I thought, "This is one big redneck." When I heard Perry preach later that morning, I thought, "This is one big redneck who is an incredible communicator." Perry Noble is an instant enigma.

Perry is a marathon runner who often waxes eloquent about the incredible desserts he devoured the night before. He is a self-described redneck who is one of the smartest, most progressive pastors in America. He honestly believes that his beloved Clemson Tigers will win the college football national championship every year even though they seldom contend for even their own conference title. And Perry is a mountain of a man who talks incessantly about his complete devotion to his wife and baby daughter. When Perry is in a room, it is impossible to miss the fact that he is there.

NewSpring, the church that Perry started in his living room, is a reflection of its unconventional pastor. NewSpring is a huge church in a small town, filled with rural Southerners worshiping God in a rock concert atmosphere. When Perry felt a desire to plant a church in 1998, he started a Bible study for college students in Anderson, South Carolina. The Bible study quickly grew from eight students to more than 150, and it became obvious that it was time to transform the informal gathering of mostly college students into what would become NewSpring Church. One hundred fifteen people attended the first official service on January 16, 2000, on the campus of Anderson College. As the church grew, it was forced to move from venue to venue on the campus until eventually it held four services every Sunday in the 1,100-seat Henderson Auditorium. More than 3,500 people were coming every weekend. In January 2006 NewSpring moved into its brand-new 2,500-seat auditorium. Attendance quickly grew to more than 7,500 people in a town of only 26,000 residents. Like Perry, NewSpring is an enigma.

I knew when I asked Perry about the first stupid mistake pastors make that he would be gut-level honest. I was not disappointed.

Why do you think pastors try to do too much themselves?

A couple of reasons automatically stick out in my mind. The first is insecurity. Many times we fear that by not doing it all, we are going to hurt someone's feelings and/or offend them. We believe that by doing, more people will have a higher view of us and thereby overlook any faults or flaws that we may have. Many of us simply need to feel needed, like we are someone's hero, and being a pastor who does it all can fulfill that area of sin in our lives.

The second reason pastors try to do too much is that we fail to teach people that the church is not effective when the pastor ministers to the people, but rather when the body ministers to the body. Many of us feel that if we teach people that God expects them to actually do ministry rather than critique it, they may leave the church. So in order not to ruffle feathers, we visit hospitals, speak at pets' funerals, eat food that we don't like with people who sometimes bother us, and change the marquee every week.

Was doing too much ever a challenge for you? What has helped you grow in this area?

Yes! I used to have this complex that said, "If I don't do it, then it will not get done correctly." So I would not delegate ministry very often; instead, I just took more and more on my plate.

The thing that helped me to grow in this area, first of all, was a better understanding of what Scripture says in Ephesians 4:11–16:

> It was he who gave some to be apostles, some to be prophets, some to be evangelists, and some to be pastors and teachers, to prepare God's people for works of service, so that the body of Christ may be built up until we all reach unity in the faith and in the knowledge of the Son of God and become mature, attaining to the whole measure of the fullness of Christ. Then we will no longer be infants, tossed back and forth by the waves, and blown here and there by every wind of teaching and by the cunning and craftiness of men in their deceitful scheming. Instead, speaking the truth in love, we will in all things grow up into him who is the Head, that is, Christ. From him the whole body, joined and held together by every supporting ligament, grows and builds itself up in love, as each part does its work.

Our calling as pastors is to train and equip people for the ministry, not to do it all for them.

The second thing was for me to repent of my pride and admit that I am not very good at many things. For me to hold all of the ministry opportunities in my hands and not challenge others to get involved was actually cheating them out of opportunities to further develop their relationship with Jesus.

Are there any areas of ministry in your church that you used to do that are being done more effectively by someone else now?

Yes! I used to lead worship and preach every Sunday. In fact, I did this for about the first six months our church was in existence. It was horrible! I probably knew about three or four chords on the guitar, and we pretty much had around ten songs in our rotation. We sang the children's song "Pharaoh, Pharaoh" one Sunday morning because I wanted to introduce a new song, but that's the only one I could play! We hired a worship leader in May of that year, and by June first he had kicked me out of the band!

I also used to do all of our media slides and presentations. I still have some of them on an old laptop computer, and they are horrible! I remember releasing that responsibility to someone else about eight months into our church plant, and the quality got better really quickly.

What are two or three keys you have found in empowering others to do the work of the ministry?

I would say the first is teaching others that to really develop a solid relationship with Jesus, there has to be an element of serving others. It is bothersome to me when people claim they "want to go deep" but have splinters in their rear ends from sitting around all day and doing nothing. Spiritual maturity is not only measured by knowledge; if that were the case, then the devil would be more spiritually mature than any pastor on the planet, because he knows way more than all of us! But maturity *is* developed when people do what Jesus did by serving others.

The second key to empowering others is to teach the church that there are many ministry opportunities that the members can do much better than I can. Many pastors like to believe that we are the best at everything in regard to ministry, and that simply is not true. There are so many things that others can do better than I ever could dream of doing them. Through teaching and encouragement of that very thing, I've discovered that people are more than willing to embrace ministry opportunities when they see that they are needed.

What advice would you give to the pastor of a smaller church who is struggling to get everything done?

You do not have to have a large staff in order to delegate ministry. There are people in your church, right now, who would get involved in a skinny minute if you would just ask them. Sure, they might not do ministry the way you would have done it; it might actually be better. I know there may be a fear that in asking them to "do" something, you may offend them, causing them to leave. Nothing could be further from the truth; in fact, I've discovered that by not asking them to assist in ministry, you are way more likely to lose quality leaders to a place where they feel as if they can make a difference.

Second, I would say to trust in God's sovereignty way more than your own ability. Way too many times I have put God to the side and not asked for his involvement in something just because of feeling so overwhelmed.

Last of all, I would say that all pastors of any church size need to realize that the church would survive without us were we to die in an accident tomorrow. Seriously, the church belongs to Jesus, not us. We are stewards — not owners. Jesus has been doing this church deal for two thousand years without us, and it will continue on after all of us are gone. She is his bride, and he will always make sure she is radiant and beautiful.

IQ Test

Take time to work through the following questions. Then share your answers with two or three trusted leaders for feedback and accountability.

1. How would you describe your leadership style? How would other leaders in your church describe you?

   a. I do most of the work myself.

   b. I have help in some areas, but I still do more than I should.

   c. I have delegated many areas, but there are still areas I need to give away.

   d. I only do the things that only I can do.

2. If your answer to question 1 is a, b, or c, why do you think you struggle giving away ministry?

3. What tasks do you currently do in your church that only you can do? What tasks do you currently do that you should give away?

4. What are some ministries or events that currently occur at your church that should simply cease to exist?

5. Name three people in your church to whom you can give away ministry, starting today. What are you going to give away first? How are you going to mentor the new steward of that area of ministry?

2

ESTABLISHING THE WRONG ROLE FOR THE PASTOR'S FAMILY

"I REALIZE THAT THE CHURCH SECRETARY CAN'T TYPE, BUT SHE'S THE MOTHER OF MY CHILDREN."

I'll never forget Easter Sunday in 1993. I had been pastoring the little church in Huffman, Texas, for about nine months. Attendance had grown from eleven adults to about seventy on an average Sunday. In January I had heard a pastor named Rick Warren (you may have heard of him) talk about how he had started Saddleback Church by sending out a mailer. I had never heard of such a thing, but I was willing to try. I purchased a mailing list and created a flyer that looked remarkably like the one Saddleback had created. (I included my picture instead of Rick's because I thought that might be confusing.) We didn't have enough money to pay someone to address and mail them, so we printed labels on our little dot matrix printer, and a small but determined group of volunteers spent a full day sticking labels on ten thousand flyers and sorting them into zip code order. We decided to put on a passion play for Easter, so we built a ginormous set that overwhelmed our little auditorium. We worked every day and most nights for a month on the set and the mailer and the passion play, praying desperately that God would honor our efforts. Finally, Easter Sunday arrived.

Cars began arriving about thirty minutes before the service was scheduled to begin. Our little gravel parking lot was soon full, and we began parking cars in the field next to the church. When that was full, we parked cars on the street. We ran out of seats about ten minutes before church began. By the time I stood up to begin the service, people were filling the little lobby and standing along the walls in the back of the auditorium. The service went very well: the passion play came off without being too cheesy, and God seemed to use the sermon to speak to people's lives. It was the largest crowd the church had ever had, and several families indicated they would definitely be back. At the end of the day, I was completely exhausted, but I couldn't have been more excited. It seemed like everything I had dreamed of, prayed for, and worked toward was coming together. I was finally seeing the vision for Church on the Lake become a reality.

On the ride home from church, I was going on and on about what a great day it had been. I noticed that my beautiful wife was very quiet, and when I looked over, I saw tears streaming down her face. I'm not real perceptive, but I picked up right away that these were not tears of joy. When I asked what was wrong, she began to pour out her heart. While this was the highlight of my ministry, she was at the lowest point of her life; "our" ministry was killing her. She was working a full-time job, raising two young children, and pouring herself into the church. She helped lead worship, she directed the children's ministry, she helped clean the church on Saturdays, and she filled in whenever someone couldn't teach a Sunday school class. In the midst of all the work and all the pressure and all the criticism that come with being a pastor's wife, she felt herself disappearing. It was my church and my ministry and my career, and she was just a player on the stage of my life. Who was Sherry? What did God create her to do? What was his vision for her life?

Sherry had tried to communicate to me before how she was being swallowed by ministry, but I had always tried to just ride out the storm and figured she'd feel better later. The truth was that I had no idea how to deal with what she was feeling. I understood mission and vision and calling. I knew how to work hard and learn as much as I could about how to do church, but I had no idea how to be the spiritual leader and protector of my family. I assumed as long as they were coming along for the ride, they would be okay.

I'd like to say that day was the end of the destructive path of ministry that I had been on since the day we were married; that I woke up to the danger of putting ministry before family and the relational devastation caused by ignoring my wife's real needs and maintaining peace on the surface, but it was really only a speed bump on the highway that almost destroyed my family. Sherry continued to play the dutiful pastor's wife, and we continued to drift apart. Eventually I left the church and took a job teaching school, thinking that would fix everything. But I still didn't understand the damage that had been done. The worst was yet to come. That day began a transition in our lives that has continued to this day. I still struggle with running as fast as I can toward what I think God is calling me to without making sure that my family is also finding fulfillment in God's unique calling on their lives.

How to Destroy Your Family

Over twenty-six years of ministry and marriage, I have discovered several stupid ways to destroy your family while pursuing God's vision for your ministry. Let me share a few.

Playing the "ministry" card. This one goes something like this: "Honey, God has called me to ministry — what else can I do? I know that being a pastor's wife is tough, but I can't say no to God." While it is hard to argue with God, it's pretty easy to resent his smug mouthpiece. My personal twist on this play was to remind Sherry that she knew I was going to be a pastor when she married me, so she knew what she was getting into. That didn't help the situation as much as you would think.

Leading with the queen of hearts. The most available volunteer in most churches is the pastor's wife. She often is called on to work in children's ministry, music ministry, and women's ministry. She is also the go-to girl when someone doesn't show up to teach Sunday school or fold bulletins or clean bathrooms. The best part is she can't say no because she is helping her husband fulfill his God-given calling. Eventually, however, she may begin to dream of substituting real blood for grape juice while filling Communion cups before the church service.

Trumping family time with ministry. Ministry can easily become a 24-7 occupation. There is always a sermon to write, a service to plan, a conference to attend, a book to read, a marriage to save, or a conflict to mediate. And Sundays seem to come every seven days. A pastor can find himself writing a sermon on the importance of quality time with the family while missing his daughter's soccer game. It's surprising how often listening to the call of God seems to lead to ignoring the cries of the pastor's own family.

Tipping the family's hand to the congregation. The best thing about being married as a pastor is that you have instant illustrations. When you are talking about the differences between men and women, the last fight you had with your wife over the budget makes a great point. ("Pastor, I really appreciate the fact that you are so transparent when you speak. You are so real.") The conversation you had last week with your son provides great insight into how teenagers think. Good thing you are in the middle of a series called "Family Ties." One tip on using your family as sermon fodder; avoid eye contact with them at all times when giving the sermon. If looks can kill, you might become a sacrificial lamb on the altar. (Or the Plexiglas pulpit, depending on your church's theology of furniture.)

Betting the family's future. The final straw in my family came when "we" made the decision to move from Texas to South Carolina. Seacoast was experiencing rapid growth, and the church offered me the chance to come on staff as Pastor of Family Ministry, a title that would become rather ironic in a few short months. I used all my powers of persuasion to get Sherry to agree to the move, and in July 1996 we loaded up a U-Haul truck and moved halfway across the country. Sherry and I had almost stopped speaking to each other by the time we arrived in Charleston. Over the next few months, our relationship deteriorated to the point that we would communicate only when absolutely necessary. Sherry missed her old job and friends, felt the move had negatively impacted our children, and didn't like anything about our new hometown. She felt manipulated and used by me and by the church. She'd had all she could take and began to make plans to leave. While I was teaching parenting classes and giving sermons on marriage at the church, I was watching as my own family continued to unravel at home.

Rebuilding the Pastor's Home

The salvation of our marriage came at its lowest point. After we had been at Seacoast for about seven months, all of the pastors were required to attend the churchwide marriage retreat. On the first day of the retreat, the leader had all of us take our spouses' hands, look them in the eye, and tell them how much we loved them. It was one of the most painful experiences I have ever had. Feeling like the entire room was watching us, Sherry and I faced each other and mouthed the empty words "I love you." There was no feeling nor any truth attached to those words that evening, and we both knew it. On day two of the retreat, the leader announced that the afternoon was free so we could spend quality time with our spouse. After lunch, all of the couples disappeared, and Sherry and I faced the prospect of an afternoon alone with each other in an empty hotel room. We sat on the couch staring at the TV. You could almost hear the tension between us, it was so palpable. Just a few days before, Sherry had packed her bags but at the last minute decided not to leave yet. Sitting there in that hotel room, we both knew we were very near the end.

Then God intervened. Overwhelmed by a feeling she didn't understand, Sherry turned to me with tears in her eyes and said, "I want to be your friend." I felt something cold and hard shatter inside of me, and I told her I wanted to be her friend as well. I took her hand and prayed that God would heal our marriage. For the first time in months we hugged, we cried, and we did what married couples do when they are in love and have hours alone in a hotel room. That afternoon we took the first step on a lifelong journey to building a healthy marriage. Let me share with you some of what we are learning.

Marriage Is about Being There

The idea that life can be divided into a neat pyramid of priorities is a myth. This idea holds that if we will simply arrange our lives according to the formula God first, family second, and ministry third, then everything will flow together smoothly. It's a great theory, but unfortunately, life doesn't work that way. First, God isn't a priority in life; God is life. He isn't more important than your family any more than air is more important than your shoes. I don't prioritize breathing; I breathe so that I live. If I have to prioritize God, put God into some sort of hierarchical to-do list, I have missed the whole concept of what it means to walk with God. When the apostle Paul spoke to the Athenians on Mars Hill, he said that "in him we live and move and have our being" (Acts 17:28).

Family and ministry don't fit neatly into categories either. There are times when family is all I do. On the days my children were born, they were not a priority carefully balanced against the demands of ministry. When my mother was dying from cancer, I didn't worry if I was spending the right percentage of time with family. Likewise, when I had the opportunity to write and direct an Easter play attended by more than ten thousand people, I couldn't help exceeding my quota of church time. Life is all-consuming and cannot be measured and weighed and prioritized in neat categories.

The key is to establish honesty, trust, and faithfulness. When you are in a season when you know that ministry will be all-consuming, you have to be honest with your family. They have to know that you will be spending extra hours over the next few days or weeks pouring everything you have into what God has placed before you. If you have made massive deposits in the trust banks of your family members by being fully present with them in the past, they will support you through this time. If, however, you are never fully present, if you are always checking your email and taking phone calls during dinner and spending your day off doing counseling, your family will not understand or care why you feel you need to focus on ministry in this season.

When you are having lunch with your wife or watching your son play soccer or talking to your daughter about school, your ministry should be completely out of bounds. No problem, no question, no opportunity should penetrate the heat shield of your family time. Your family and your congregation have to know that when you are with family, you are available only to them. The future of your marriage and family depends on it.

Sherry and I have declared "Seacoast-free zones." When we have a date night, we will agree in advance that we will not discuss anything about the church or people in the church. (We also have "children-free zones," times when neither of us can talk about the kids. Those zones tend to be rather quiet.) Last year we bought a boat and decreed it a permanent Seacoast-free zone. Each of us also has permission to put a moratorium on any talk associated with the church at any time. These measures help us to draw boundaries and create space for ourselves outside the often all-consuming ministry.

Marriage Is Also about Not Being There

Another great way we have found to keep sanity in our marriage and family while working in a very demanding ministry environment is to run away on a frequent basis. As often as possible, Sherry and I pack a bag and take off for the weekend. Sometimes we take the kids with us, and sometimes we abandon them. (They are currently seventeen and twenty-one, so we aren't breaking any laws when we sneak out of town.) One of the best places we have found to escape is Fairhaven Ministries (www.fairhavenministries.net), a beautiful retreat center made up of individual cabins set in the Smoky Mountains of Tennessee. They offer cabins to full-time pastors for $50 per night and an escape from the grind of ministry that is priceless. We make sure we get away to Fairhaven for at least two or three days every year.

You and your spouse need regular mini-retreats. Even if it just involves driving to the next town and staying in the Motel 6, one of the keys to sanity in ministry is to escape together. When our kids were younger and we had a day off, we would throw a tent in the back of the car and head to the mountains together. It rained every single time we went, and I never did figure out the right way to set up the tent, but for a few hours every few months, we were away from ministry and together as a family. How long has it been since you jumped in the minivan and headed for the hills? It's time to do it again.

Sometimes Marriage Is about Getting Help

A funny thing about pastors is that when they need to fix their car, they go to a mechanic, and when they need to fix their health, they go to a doctor, but when their marriage needs help, they are almost never willing to go to an expert for help. I know a pastor who has been struggling in his marriage for as long as I have known him. I've heard him advise other couples to meet with a professional to get help with their marriage, but anytime I mention that he and his wife could use a counselor, he finds an excuse not to go. It's almost as if he'd rather suffer than admit he needs help.

Sherry and I have gone to Christian marriage counselors on several occasions. Some of them have been very helpful, others not so much. But every time we have talked to a counselor, the experience has helped us open up and talk to each other. It's as if we need an outside party to pry the lid off our conversation and allow us to get to the real truth. Fairhaven Ministries, which I mentioned earlier, offers great counseling for pastors and their families at a very reasonable rate. Good Christian counselors can be found all over the country. If your marriage is struggling, don't hesitate to pick up the phone and admit you need help. Of all the stupid mistakes a pastor can make, not getting help with his marriage is the dumbest of all.

The Key to Your Marriage Is at Home

This weekend take your wife out for a nice dinner. If you have children at home, arrange for a babysitter. (Don't ask your wife to do it; you can figure this one out, big guy.) Ask your wife about her day. Reminisce with her about the past, when you met, when you fell in love, when you got married. Ask her if life is turning out the way she thought it would. Then drop the bomb: "How is the church impacting you and our family?" Listen to what she says and what she doesn't say. Don't correct her or argue with her, but ask her to explain and illustrate when you do not understand. Don't try to fix problems or find solutions; just listen. When she has shared her heart, ask if you can pray with her that God will help the two of you build a strong marriage and family together. Buy her something chocolate for dessert and begin to plan your next family escape. My prayer for you is that you will build a marriage as rich and fulfilling as mine is today.

For a fresh perspective on prioritizing family and ministry, I talked to my friend Chris Hodges, who pastors Church of the Highlands in Birmingham, Alabama. With five children — four boys and one girl — Chris and his wife, Tammy, do a phenomenal job of balancing family and ministry.

·················· **SPOTLIGHT** ·················

Chris Hodges, Church of the Highlands

My first meeting with Chris Hodges did not go well. Seacoast was talking with Chris about helping him start Church of the Highlands in Birmingham, Alabama, and we decided to set up a golf outing to get better acquainted. (During the spring in Charleston, a surprising number of meetings conclude with the phrase, "Why don't we discuss this over a round of golf?") I ended up being paired with Chris in the same golf cart. This arrangement was not good. I did not realize until about the fifth hole that Chris is a very good golfer and very serious about the game. I was a very poor golfer (I have since retired from the game) and not at all serious about the game. After several attempts at lame humor, I realized that I was the only one laughing; it turns out that stand-up comedy and a great putting round don't really go together. Chris was very polite, but we both knew that being golf buddies probably wasn't in our future. At the end of the round (Chris beat me by about forty strokes), we shook hands and agreed never to play golf together again. (Not verbally, but it was implied.)

Over the next few months, I watched as Chris carried the same focus and determination from the golf course into church planting. In February 2001 he and a group of thirty-four volunteers, his "Dream Team," planted Church of the Highlands. Focusing on reaching out to unchurched people by building relational small groups throughout the city, Church of the Highlands grew to more than six hundred attendees by the end of 2001, helped plant six other churches, and gave nearly one-quarter of its income to missions. Church of the Highlands has now grown to more than eight thousand weekly attendees in four locations, making it one of the fastest-growing churches in North America.

One of the most impressive things about the growth at Church of the Highlands has been Chris's ability to keep his focus on his family. In the midst of the craziness of planting a church, moving in and out of a temporary location every seven days, and ministering to the needs of hundreds of new people showing up every weekend, Chris has managed to keep his eye on the ball; the real reflection of the success that Chris has found is in his family. So I asked Chris to give us some good pointers on improving our game at home.

How important has your spouse been in the success of your ministry?

My wife, Tammy, has never been one who wanted to be "public" in her ministry. She always considered her greatest gift and contribution to be a wife to me and a mother to the kids. And the result is, other than my relationship with God, my family is the stabilizing force of my life. With the family life solid and strong, it enables me to do all that God has called me to do.

Have you struggled balancing ministry and family? How have you been able to grow in this area?

It was tough at first when we were planting the church because we did everything — took every phone call, etc. But I have always had at least one night a week dedicated as a "date night" and one night a week dedicated as a "family night." The greatest revelation I ever got about this, however, was not to have two worlds — ministry and family. Instead of compartmentalizing, the two were integrated. We do ministry together as a family — traveling the world together. I get ideas from my kids about messages and share stories and testimonies about changed lives around the dinner table.

How have you helped your children deal with the demands placed on pastors' kids?

I think it begins with me. I haven't placed any special demands on my kids or ever pressured them to act a certain way because they were my kids. In turn, no one in our church has placed any special demands on them. They all serve in the areas that they are passionate about just like everyone else in the church.

What mistakes do you see other pastors making when it comes to dealing with their family and ministry?

The biggest mistake is neglecting our families for the sake of the ministry. But like I said earlier, you can't have two worlds. The best thing to do in my opinion is to do church life with your family — get their advice, share in the struggles and blessings of ministry, take them along as travel companions on ministry trips, etc. The result for us is our kids feel fortunate that they are in a ministry home. They think they have advantages that no other children have.

What practical advice would you give to the pastor of a small church who is struggling to balance the demands of the ministry and care for his family?

Get the family involved. When we began our church, my kids, at the time ages eleven and nine, duplicated and labeled over one hundred cassette tapes that were ordered from the previous week's message. They had more fun and felt like they were a part of the ministry with me. But here's another thought: anytime a pastor is "too busy," it's because he hasn't spent enough time giving ministry away to others. So it doesn't matter whether or not the church is small or large — give ministry away and you'll have plenty of time to do the things that only you can do — study, spend time with family, etc.

IQ Test

When you have finished reading this chapter, take the following IQ Test. Then ask your spouse to read the chapter and take the test. Finally, hire a babysitter and go out for a quiet evening together to compare notes from the quiz and to plan next steps to continue building or to begin rebuilding your marriage.

1. How would you describe your spouse's role in your ministry?
   a. She works in the area of her gifting.
   b. She fills whatever role is most needed in the church.
   c. She isn't really involved in the ministry at the church.
   d. She resents the ministry.

2. How would your spouse answer this question: "How is the church impacting you and our family?"

3. How do your children feel about your ministry? How do they feel toward your church?

4. Are you regularly building into your marriage and family? When was the last time you surprised your wife with a weekend away from church? How long has it been since you loaded up the minivan and went camping with the family?

5. Is there another couple in ministry outside of your church with whom you can connect for fellowship and mentoring? Would it be beneficial to talk with a Christian counselor about your marriage?

3

PROVIDING A SECOND-RATE WORSHIP EXPERIENCE

"THE PIANO PLAYER'S NOT GREAT,
BUT SHE KEEPS BETTER TIME THAN THE DRUMMER."

Before I became the pastor at Church on the Lake, I had lunch with Rob, the former pastor. Rob was a sharp young man who seemed beaten down by two years of leading this small flock in Huffman, Texas. He had been called as pastor after a particularly acrimonious split in which accusations of improprieties flew in every direction. (There's nothing nastier than a small church split.) For two years he tried to heal wounds and mend fences while the church continued to shrink. Rob said that anyone with get-up-and-go finally got up and went. When he finally reached the end of his rope and was ready to let someone else take a swing at it, I was the lucky winner.

One of my main goals in talking to Rob was to discover what kinds of gifts the remaining members possessed. I knew the church was small, but maybe there were still diamonds in the rough. Rob sighed and explained that while the people were mostly good-hearted (I would find out later what he meant by "mostly"), there wasn't a lot of talent left.

"What about the musicians?" I asked.

"Well, there's Estelle, who plays the piano. She does okay if you stick to songs in the hymnal and don't change keys. Ernesto enjoys playing the drums. Oh, and Bob shows up once in a while to play the guitar."

"So mostly it's just drums and piano?"

Rob nodded yes. I could tell by the pained look on his face that this wasn't his favorite subject. He was the worship leader, and his little band didn't seem to bring him any joy.

"How do they sound?"

There was a long pause while Rob searched for a gentle answer. Finally, he said, "Well, the piano player has better rhythm than the drummer."

I knew we had a problem. For the next two and a half years we struggled each weekend to provide a worship experience that would honor the name of God and not cause undue damage to the body. Some days we succeeded; most days we came up short. On one acutely painful Sunday, we arrived at the church to find that we had no electricity.

This discovery was particularly disturbing because we were still in our karaoke worship phase, so acoustic wasn't a possibility. In the end we sat in a cold, dark auditorium singing worship songs accompanied by a battery-powered boom box. In order for the congregation to hear the music, I sat on the front row and held the tape player above my head. I'd like to say it was an amazing God moment when we learned that all we needed to worship were willing hearts, but it wasn't. It was just kind of pitiful.

In the years since then, I have learned a lot about what does and does not work in creating a great weekend worship service. Let's look at ten ways (batteries included) you can improve the weekend service at your church.

Ten Easy (Sort of) Ways to Improve Your Weekend Experience

1. Ask the Hard Questions

Have you ever asked why you have a Sunday morning service? Other than on Sunday afternoon when you are thinking, "Why do I do this? Please, God, let me do something else." That's just PPSS (post-preaching stress syndrome). We all have it. Just watch some football or NASCAR or violent movies until it goes away. The hard questions we all need to ask are these: "What is the purpose of having a service every Sunday morning? What are we trying to accomplish?" It's amazing that we do the same thing every weekend, week after week, year after year, and yet we seldom sit down to ask why we are doing it.

There is no way to improve our Sunday services until we know why we are having church. And our reasons need to be razor sharp. Are you there to carry on a tradition? Is your main focus to feed the saints who show up every weekend? Are you trying to entertain visitors who may or may not come back next week? Or are you driven by a desire to make God famous and to bring honor to his name whatever it takes?

If the purpose of your Sunday morning service is to make God famous, is it happening? Does everything you do on a Sunday morning bring honor to God? Would he be proud of the way your building looks when he drives into the parking lot? Is your music something that would bring joy to his heart if he were sitting in the front row? What about the sermon you preached last weekend? Would God say, "Wow, he really did everything he possibly could to build my reputation through that message"? If God brought his friends to church, would he be proud to show them what you are doing to bring glory to his name? Does God brag about your church to the angels?

We often give lip service to the concept of honoring God on Sunday mornings. Sometimes we're even a little self-righteous about the fact that we don't worry about externals — we're more focused on the spiritual. But how can a shoddy weekend experience honor a God who created the Rocky Mountains and the Pacific Ocean and Diet Coke? (Okay, Diet Coke is a reach, but you get the idea.) While the end product will look very different from church to church, if we really want to make God's name famous, we have to give our very best effort in everything we do every Sunday.

Another hard question to ask is "Who are we trying to reach?" The target audience of some churches is the whole world. The problem is that the whole world doesn't live two doors down from the church. The apostle Paul used a very targeted approach to ministry: "To the Jews I became like a Jew, to win the Jews. To those under the law I became like one under the law (though I myself am not under the law), so as to win those under the law. To those not having the law I became like one not having the law (though I am not free from God's law but am under Christ's law), so as to win those not having the law. To the weak I became weak, to win the weak. I have become all things to all men so that by all possible means I might save some" (1 Cor. 9:20 – 22).

Who has God placed in your path and called you to reach with the good news? The answer to that question will have big implications for what your Sunday services will look like. We are currently struggling with this question at one of our Seacoast campuses located in a growing Hispanic community in Charleston. When we walk around the neighborhood, we hear Latino music coming from the cars and trailers in the community; we don't play Latino music on Sunday mornings. The challenge is that we don't know how to play Latino music. If we are called to reach our community and our community is listening to Latino music, do we try to get them to change their music so they will come to our church, or do we change our music to try to relate to them? Call me if you know of a good mariachi worship band in the greater Charleston area.

One of the ways I like to figure out who we need to reach is to hang out at Starbucks on Sunday mornings. Once the church attendees clear out (they are the ones wearing ties and looking uptight), I find myself surrounded by people who don't wake up each weekend thinking about Sunday school. This is the harvest field Jesus talked about. These are the people we need to reach.

So I settle in with a fake cup of coffee (I don't drink the stuff — it stunts your growth) and start taking note of the people around me. How old are the other customers? How are they dressed? What are they talking about? What kind of music are they listening to? Are they married? How old are their children? You will be amazed how much you can learn about your community sipping a tall nonfat chai latte and doing some holy eavesdropping. Once I've gathered my data, I compare it to our church on Sundays. Are we applying the timeless truth of the gospel to what the people at Starbucks are talking about? Does our church seem as accessible as Starbucks? If the people I saw at Starbucks were to drop by our church, would they fit in? Try skipping church and going to Starbucks next Sunday and see what you can learn about your community. If your community isn't a Starbucks kind of place, choose another business where people hang out on Sunday morning instead of going to church. (I hear McDonald's serves a mean cup of coffee these days.)

2. See Your Service through the Eyes of the First-Time Attender

Chip and Dan Heath, in their book *Made to Stick*, introduce an interesting concept they call the Curse of Knowledge[1]. The basic idea is you can't not know what you already know; and once you know it, it's very difficult to remember what it's like not to know. I experienced this phenomenon recently at the Department of Motor Vehicles (DMV).

I had purchased a used vehicle out of state and needed to get it registered in South Carolina. I had no idea how the process works, but I suspected it involved some form of bureaucratic magic. So I grabbed every piece of paper that somehow referenced the vehicle in question and headed to the local Department of Motor Vehicles. When I arrived, the clerk took a look at my stack of papers and handed me another stack to fill out. When they called my number, I took both stacks of incomprehensible documents to the counter. The DMV employee asked me what I wanted to do. When I told her I needed a license plate and a title, she looked at me like I had slapped her favorite baby seal. "You cannot have a title today," she said. "You'll have to wait ten days." Chagrined and ashamed of my ignorance, I stared blankly across the counter. "So what do you want to do?" she asked again. We were at an impasse; she knew how to do that special magic that makes a car legal to drive in South Carolina, but I didn't know the correct way to ask her to make it happen.

After several moments of uncomfortable silence, I finally explained that I had no idea what I wanted to do. All I knew was that I had a car I needed to make legal in the Palmetto State. I had brought all of my papers and a credit card to the DMV and was willing to give her both if she would give me one of those little stickers that kept our state's finest from giving me a ticket. She took my meager offerings and began typing my life story into a computer. She stared at the screen, stared at my paperwork, stared at the screen, and then without saying a word disappeared into one of the offices located behind the counter. After an absence of several minutes, she reappeared and told me to pay her several hundred dollars. She then handed me the sticky little rectangle of license plate freedom and told me to have a nice day.

The Curse of Knowledge — I knew too little and she knew too much. All day every day she registers cars and doles out titles (after a ten-day wait apparently), but she cannot relate to someone who doesn't understand the process. She doesn't remember what it's like not to know.

Imagine walking into your church for the first time. Maybe you have never been in a church before, or maybe this is the first time in many, many years. Imagine listening to the music, hearing the sermon. Imagine feeling a tug on your heart and knowing you need to do something to be somehow connected with God, but you have no idea what you should do or how you should do it. Imagine hearing about "small groups" and "Bible fellowship" and "baptism." Imagine having someone tell you that you need to "ask Jesus into your heart so you can be saved" and wondering what in the world that is all about.

Many of us have been in the church so long we have completely lost touch with what it's like not to know. Things like Communion, public prayer, and the collection of an offering seem very normal to us, but they can be quite intimidating to the uninitiated. If we want to improve our ability to connect with "outsiders," we have to find a way to see Sunday through their eyes.

One way to get a fresh perspective is to ask new attendees for their feedback. At Seacoast we send all those who identify themselves as new attendees a postcard and ask for their input on the service they attended. This process has been invaluable over time as we have learned things about ourselves we didn't know. For instance, we heard again and again that the newcomers liked our worship service but felt that our congregation wasn't friendly. We thought we were very friendly, but we realized we were only friendly to people we already knew. We responded by challenging our people to become "guerilla greeters" and spend the first five minutes and the last five minutes of every weekend talking to people they hadn't met before. Over the next few months, first-time attendees began to remark on the friendliness of our congregation.

Another way to get fresh insight into what it's like to visit your church is to solicit input from other churches. Over the past several years, we've had pastors from all over the country visit us at Seacoast and have found them to be invaluable in helping us look at what we do from an outsider's perspective. A team from a large church on the West Coast whose name rhymes with Paddleback helped us improve the way we handled security. We'd had some scary incidents over the past few months, so we had hired an off-duty police officer to be present during our Sunday services. The "Paddleback" team said that when they drove up and saw the police car parked up front and a uniformed officer standing at the front door, they assumed some crime had been committed. (The sermon wasn't great that weekend, but I wouldn't call it a crime.) Rather than safety and security, the presence of the police officer sparked a feeling of fear as people approached the sanctuary. Fear and trembling before a holy God is a good thing; fear and trembling crossing the parking lot is not a good thing. Acting on their advice, we asked the policeman to park in the back and to wear plain clothes in the future. Now you may enter Seacoast without fear of arrest.

To get input from another church, offer to trade pulpits with a local pastor for a week. After you have preached at each other's churches, get together and compare notes. Encourage your pastor friend to be ruthless; it's the only way you can learn. And who knows? He may agree to make the trade permanent. Then he can fix your mess.

Something we've tried lately at Seacoast is to use a secret shopper service. For a relatively small fee, a company will send a secret shopper to your church for a Sunday service. The company will then send a report to you about the secret shopper's experience. Now, I know there can be a high "ick" factor to paying someone to come to your church and getting anonymous feedback as though you are some kind of fast-food religion store. Here's the way I see it: McDonald's feels that selling hamburgers is so important that they will pay people to rate them on how well they do it. I feel that making an effective presentation of the gospel is so important that I'm willing to pay people to give me feedback on how well we do it. Having said that, I know the use of a secret shopper service is not for everyone, but it's another tool in the tool kit for becoming more effective at reaching people for Jesus.

3. Improve Your Music

Good worship music is one of the most effective means we have of helping people connect with God, and poor worship music is one of the most effective ways of keeping people from making that connection. One of the changes I knew I had to make immediately at Church on the Lake involved the worship music. Within a few weeks of becoming the pastor at the church, I had identified some amazing vocalists with hearts for worship, but our musicians were killing our services. The pianist was adequate at best and could play only a limited list of songs. The drummer used the exact same beat for every song but varied tempo wildly even within a verse. As I shared in chapter 1, when the pianist called one Saturday to say she wouldn't be able to play that weekend, I jumped at the chance to revamp the music. We found some instrumental backup tracks to some of the worship songs we were singing and launched the first all-karaoke worship team. For the next two years we didn't have a single live musician. This style of worship wasn't great, but it was much better than the alternative. Bad worship music can be lethal to a church that wants to grow.

It's interesting that when King David was preparing to bring the ark of the covenant to Jerusalem, one of the first things he did was put together a great band with a talented worship leader: "David told the leaders of the Levites to appoint their brothers as singers to sing joyful songs, accompanied by musical instruments: lyres, harps and cymbals.... Kenaniah the head Levite was in charge of the singing; that was his responsibility because he was skillful at it" (1 Chron. 15:16, 22).

The second most vital leader in any church is the worship leader. This person, more than anyone but the senior pastor, determines the quality and direction of the Sunday service. The importance of music in worship is stressed over and over again in the Psalms and throughout the Old Testament. It is obvious that God loves a great worship band.

One of the keys to finding and keeping a great worship leader and band is to realize that musicians are wired differently than others. God made them creative, and their creativity doesn't always happen between 9:00 a.m. and 5:00 p.m. (There are exceptions, but most great worship leaders I've been around don't realize that there are two 9:00s in a day.) There is biblical precedent to treating musicians differently than other workers: "Those who were musicians, heads of Levite families, stayed in the rooms of the temple and were exempt from other duties because they were responsible for the work day and night" (1 Chron. 9:33).

When you find the right worship leader and the right musicians, be prepared to treat them differently than your youth leader or your administrative assistant. There's a good chance the artists who lead worship in your church thrive at 2:00 a.m. but are completely ineffective before 10:00 a.m. Learn the rhythms of their lives and allow them to be the individuals God created them to be. Their work hours may not match everyone else's schedule, a fact that won't thrill the accountant types on your team who feel that everyone should clock in at 8:00 a.m., ready to work with sharpened #2 pencil in hand. When they complain, offer to have the artists trade jobs with them; next month the accountant types can lead worship and the artists will keep the books. I'm fairly sure they'll see it your way after that.

Another factor to consider when building a great worship team is the possibility of paying your musicians. It's ironic to me that we think it is normal to pay the pastor, the administrative assistant, the children's director, and the youth director, but when we talk about paying musicians, some people are outraged. "We don't pay ushers or greeters or Sunday school teachers — why should we pay a guitar player?" When your church needs insurance, do you pay a professional insurance company, or do you ask for a volunteer from the members who might want to try their hand at liability insurance? Which is more important in helping us lead people into the presence of God: insurance or musicians?

When Seacoast adopted a struggling church plant in Columbia, South Carolina, one of the major changes we made was to give the worship leader permission to pay some musicians. He was an exceptionally talented worship leader, but he had been struggling for years working with an all-volunteer band. He brought in some of his talented friends, and the attendance at the church doubled almost instantly. We began to see people reconnect with God and others meet God for the first time as they were ushered into his presence by a man with a gift from God surrounded by talented musicians whom we paid to help us reach the world for Jesus.

Your town probably has some very capable musicians who are struggling to make a living with their instruments. You will find them playing late-night gigs in local bars and restaurants, trying out new instruments at the music store, or taking music classes at the community college. You could be a blessing in their lives and at the same time expand the reach of your church simply by paying them for a few hours' work on a Sunday.

When you decide to improve the quality of your music, however, you will face opposition from those who may be displaced by the change. It's important to help people see how God has actually gifted them and how they can use their gifts to further the kingdom. While your current guitar player may not have the skill to play on Sunday mornings, he may very well be an excellent small group worship leader. Be careful when making these kinds of changes to honor the gifts and feelings of those the change is hardest on, but also not to let the feelings of one or two preclude ministry to many, many more.

When we changed the music at Church on the Lake, both the piano player and the drummer eventually left to attend other churches. Over time, however, we were able to lead many people into a relationship with Christ who might never have made it through Estelle and Ernesto's first horrendous performance.

4. Update Your Technology

Sometimes when we talk about updating technology, people will say that Paul didn't need the latest technology to spread the gospel. I think Paul did use the best technology available at the time. He did not write his letters on stone tablets or paint them on cave walls. He often traveled by ship or by horseback rather than by foot. I believe that if Paul lived in the twenty-first century, he would have a blog detailing his missionary journeys, stream his sermons on the internet, and send pastoral emails to the churches in Asia. When he said that he used all means possible so that he might save some, I can't help but believe that would include cutting-edge technology.

The downside of technology is that it always costs a little more than you want to pay. Keep in mind two important guidelines when you look at making upgrades: know your budget and know your priorities. No matter how little you are able to spend, you can always improve something. For instance, $50 will buy a better instrument cable that should stop that incessant buzz in the speakers; $500 will net a subwoofer to give the music some thump; $5,000 will pay for a good video projector bright enough to see even in daylight; $50,000 will replace your sound system, get a good-quality video projector and computer, and buy a decent theatrical lighting system; and $500,000 will cover lots of cool toys for the video team to play with. (Video is an expensive habit.) The important thing is to decide how much you can spend before you sit down with the salesperson.

You also need to decide your technology priorities in advance. At Seacoast we try to stick to a fairly basic set of priorities based on how we do ministry: audio, video, lighting. We always want our service to sound good, so we put the bulk of our technology dollars into improving how our services sound to the congregation. We are also a very video-driven ministry, so we focus on having a bright, clear image on the screen. Finally, we want to be able to light the stage in a creative way and to control the amount of light, so we put the rest of our technology budget into theatrical lighting in all of our venues.

While the best technology in the world will never win someone to Christ, bad technology can erect barriers between the gospel presentation and the outsider in the pew. Be sure to find the money in the budget to tear those barriers down.

5. Overhaul Your Preaching

A principal way to improve your weekend service is to improve the preaching of the Word. God uses the foolishness of preaching, but that doesn't mean preaching needs to be foolish. One of the greatest privileges in life is to be allowed to stand on a stage and present the gospel to an audience. That is a bigger deal than winning a Super Bowl, becoming the president, or singing in a rock band. If you plan to preach next Sunday, you should be working on getting better at it this week.

The way to begin improving your preaching is to watch and listen to yourself. I know it's painful and there are some things you just don't want to know, but the reality is that if your people have to sit through your sermons, you should too. A great preaching tool I've found is the video iPod. Every week Seacoast posts our messages on iTunes, where they can be downloaded for free. Every time I preach, I download the message the next week and critique myself. Doing so was difficult at first, but as I've gotten used to it, I've found several areas where I can improve my preparation and delivery.

A second way to improve your preaching is to have skilled speakers critique your messages as often as possible. Your spouse may not be a good source for this critique. Every time I preach, my wife tells me I did a great job. In twenty-six years of marriage, she has told me

I did well almost every time. When she told me after one particularly terrible sermon, "Well, it wasn't your best," I knew I probably should leave town. Find another pastor who will listen to your messages and give you feedback, or find one or two people in the church who will help you work on improving. Just make sure they understand that they need to withhold their criticism until Monday afternoon. Anything earlier could prove fatal.

A third way to improve your preaching is to listen to other pastors from around the country. Podcasts have been one of the best inventions to come along for pastors. Every week I listen to a pastor in Washington, a pastor in Texas, and a pastor in Georgia. Sometimes I borrow some of their ideas, but mostly I am learning from their style and delivery how I can become more effective. Take lessons from some of the best preachers in the country. The best part is that it's free. You can get started by clicking on "Podcasts" in the iTunes music store and selecting "Religion and Spirituality." You will find hundreds of pastors from all over the country.

A fourth, radical way to improve the preaching at your church is to get someone else to do it. You may be a lousy preacher but a great pastor who should pass the teaching responsibility off to someone else. Some churches, such as Heartland Community Church in Rockford, Illinois, don't even have a teaching pastor. Until recently Heartland simply played a video of the teaching at another church and focused on the other aspects of ministry.

At the very least you should form a preaching team. This kind of team offers several benefits. First, it develops the gift of preaching in other leaders in your church. Second, it allows your congregation to experience a variety of voices and perspectives. Some people in your church will connect more readily with another teacher while still recognizing you as the senior pastor. Finally, a preaching team will give you a break. Once in a while it's great to have a week to focus on areas besides sermon preparation and to have more than one week to study for an upcoming message. Having a team will make you a better preacher.

6. Get Creative

Americans don't do boring. They will put up with heresy, lies, and deception; but if you bore them, they will check out immediately. It is not the purpose of church to entertain the congregation, but if we don't engage their imaginations, we will never reach them. Americans are bombarded all day every day by creative media coming from every direction. To cut through the noise, we have to get creative.

Jesus was never boring. He used visual illustrations whenever he taught: "Consider the lilies of the field," "I will make you fishers of men," "I am the Good Shepherd." Jesus used current events such as the fall of the tower in Siloam to bring his point home. One of the most creative object lessons ever taught was Jesus' feeding of five thousand men with five loaves of bread and two fish. Every child who has been to Sunday school remembers that story.

While replicating Jesus' miracles to spice up your sermons might be a tall order, you can certainly add creativity to your weekend services. No matter how gifted your imagination, you should surround yourself with a creative team. Many people in your congregation have creative gifts that they would love to use to expand the kingdom if they had the chance. Mitch and Rebecca at Seacoast's Greenville campus are a great example. Mitch is an architect and Rebecca is an interior designer, and both are exceptionally talented artists. Each time Seacoast creates a new sermon series, Mitch and Rebecca design a new stage set for their campus. They then lead a team of volunteers who do all of the painting and installation. Because their pastor has released Mitch and Rebecca to use their creative gifts, every weekend visitors to Seacoast Greenville are intrigued by an imaginative backdrop that visually reinforces the sermon of the day.

Another way we use the creative gifts of our congregation is in preparing our sermons. Once we have the basic concept for the sermon for the weekend, we take the outline to what we call the creative team (pretty clever, huh?). They then look for ways we could illustrate the message with original videos, film clips, drama, or other media that would reinforce the message. Some of the ideas that have come from this team include preaching from the front seat of a Jeep, riding a motorcycle onstage, and hitting golf balls into the audience during a message on mulligans. People tend to remember a message when they've had to dodge Titleists coming at them at over 100 miles per hour. (We actually used Wiffle balls, but the audience didn't know that until after the fact.) Someone stopped me this week and mentioned that sermon, which we did almost five years ago. You may never fire projectiles at your parishioners, but you can improve the weekend experience at your church simply by gathering a team of creative crazies and turning them loose working on next Sunday's service.

7. Do Everything on Purpose

The most valuable sixty to ninety minutes of the week are the minutes when your congregation is sitting in the pews or chairs in your auditorium. Every single minute is valuable and nothing should be done without planning and without a specific purpose.

How many times have you made this announcement: "The children's ministry is looking for volunteers in the nursery. If you would be willing to help, please talk to Mary Smith after the service"? How many times has that announcement been effective? If the announcement works, why do you have to make it over and over again? The reality is that announcements only remind people to do something they are already thinking about, and no one in your congregation is sitting in church on Sunday thinking, "I sure hope the children's ministry is desperate for nursery workers. I'd really like to go wipe a baby's butt this morning." The reality is that we don't make the plea for volunteers because we think it will help; we do it so the children's ministry director will leave us alone. Likewise, people volunteer when someone personally invites them, not when they hear a plea from the pulpit. If we are going to improve our weekend services, we have to make sure everything we do from the platform is purposeful. Pleading for volunteers doesn't make the cut.

Another rule at Seacoast is that nothing gets announced if it impacts less than 25 percent of the audience. If Sister Busybody's quilting bee is canceling its Thursday meeting because of Sister Blabbermouth's goiter operation, they can just call each other. We don't make personal references to people most of the congregation don't know; we don't announce that a blue Ford Escort, license plate IMA-NUT, still has its lights on (we have jumper cables); and we don't plug upcoming ministry events just to build a crowd. We get a lot of flack from leaders who feel that their ministry desperately needs a push from the pulpit, but that's not the purpose of the Sunday morning service. Every minute is precious and every word has to count.

Another way to make sure that every element of the weekend service is purposeful is to cut the palaver to a minimum. Most of us waste far too much time on meaningless chatter. We tell stories that have no point, we fill time with meaningless Christianese, and we repreach the sermon that everyone just heard. When I was in Bible college, a guest speaker gave us great advice for a Sunday service: "Stand up, speak up, shut up."

A great exercise to streamline your weekend service is to sit down with a team immediately following Sunday morning and analyze everything that was said and done. What was the one thing we wanted people to walk away with this weekend? Why did we make that announcement? Could that information be communicated more effectively in another way? Why did we sing that song? Did it enhance the message of the weekend? Did the people leave with a clear vision of what they should do in light of the gospel, or did we send them out with five places to sign up and three events to attend?

8. Pay Attention to the Clock

A lot of churches could improve their Sunday experience by learning to tell time. If you say that your church service starts at 11:00 a.m., then it should start at 11:00 a.m. When you start services late, you do two things: you train your people to come later and later, and you tick off new people who show up on time. If an engineer decides to visit your church next Sunday, he will arrive at 10:55 a.m. He will be in his seat and ready for church to start at 10:59. If you have not started by 11:04, he will have already decided not to come back. He will assume since you do not care about his time, you do not care about him. Nothing you do after 11:05 will reach the engineer, the banker, or the business owner. They live their lives by the clock and they expect you to do the same. It sounds simplistic, but just starting on time can help your church grow.

As important as starting when you say you start is ending your services on time. My dad used to say that the human mind can only absorb what the human behind can endure. Americans have short attention spans. They are trained to watch television shows that go to commercial every ten minutes, listen to songs that last less than four minutes, and eat food that is nuked in two minutes. Your church services can last as long as you want, but newcomers will check out somewhere between sixty and ninety minutes.

9. Warm Up Your Atmosphere

In Hawaii, state employees are required by law to exhibit the "Aloha spirit" (Hawaii Revised Statutes, section 5-7.5) by "thinking and emoting good feelings to others." When you walk onto the campus of New Hope Leeward in Honolulu, you experience this Aloha spirit as they welcome you into their 'ohana (family). Everywhere you go you are welcomed by smiling volunteers who seem genuinely happy to see you. In the lobby you are overwhelmed by the smell of brewing coffee and a hot breakfast buffet prepared each weekend for the more than three thousand attendees. Pastor Mike Lwin and his staff have created a warm, friendly atmosphere that beckons you back again and again.

How can you warm up the atmosphere at your church? Are people greeted by a smiling face as they drive into your parking lot? Are they welcomed by friendly volunteers as they enter the building? Does your lobby feel warm and inviting, a place you'd like to hang out if you had the time? Do you set a tone of fun and acceptance before the service begins?

10. Make Your Sunday Service the Most Important Thing You Do

Sunday morning should be the most important thing you do all week. Everything else you and your staff are involved in should be subordinate to the Sunday service. Anything that is competing with or taking away from Sunday needs to be eliminated. Sunday is your one shot during the week to speak truth to most of your congregation and to share the gospel with newcomers who desperately need to know Jesus.

I was talking recently with a young pastor who was frustrated because his church was not growing. He said the biggest frustration was his inability to get volunteers Sunday morning, especially in the children's ministry. He said they had an excellent Wednesday night program with talented volunteer leaders; many weeks they had more children on Wednesday night than on Sunday morning. I encouraged him to transition the Wednesday night program to Sunday mornings. I explained it would be almost impossible, with the size of his congregation, to grow on Sunday and continue to pour people's limited time, talent, and treasure into Wednesday nights. As painful as it would be, he needed to kill Wednesday nights to keep the focus on Sunday mornings. A year later his church still hasn't broken one hundred in weekend attendance, but it continues to maintain its Wednesday programs.

In this chapter we have focused on the externals of creating a meaningful worship experience for your congregation. A more basic question is whether you are leading your people to worship God in spirit and in truth — are you experiencing the power and presence of God in your weekend services? If we nail all ten of the suggestions in this chapter but are not making space in our services for our people to truly connect with God, we have missed the mark.

For fresh insight on a creative worship experience that connects people with God, I turned to Mark Batterson, founding pastor of National Community Church in Washington, D.C. Mark has quickly acquired a reputation as one of the most creative minds in the American church today, so let's find out what Mark says about creating a fresh worship experience in our weekend services.

························**SPOTLIGHT**····················

Mark Batterson, National Community Church

I have never seen Mark Batterson when he isn't smiling. When I read his blog (www.evotional.com) or listen to his podcast, I can almost hear him smiling through the internet. Mark is one of those guys everyone seems to know and everyone seems to like. If Mark had not become a pastor, I think he would have been a good choice to negotiate peace in the Middle East; everyone would want to be on his side.

I don't know if Mark was smiling when he started National Community Church (NCC) during a record-setting blizzard on January 7, 1996. Mark, his wife, and their son were the only brave souls to show up that freezing Sunday morning in the nation's capital. Typical of Mark's eternal optimism, he reports that the church grew by over 600 percent when nineteen people came the following weekend. Times remained tough that first year at NCC as the church grew to a core group of twenty-five and eventually lost its home when the public school it was meeting in was suddenly shut down. In November 1996 the church moved into the movie theater in the basement of Union Station, and a new vision for NCC was born.

In describing a church that meets in a theater in a mall, Mark says, "Our goal is to be a church for the unchurched, so I can't imagine a more strategic spiritual beachhead than Union Station. Doing church in the middle of the marketplace is part of our spiritual DNA." NCC's vision is to meet in movie theaters throughout the metro D.C. area. It currently has four locations, including Ebenezers, the largest coffee shop on Capitol Hill that NCC opened in the spring of 2006. About 73 percent of

NCC's attendees are single twentysomethings, and 70 percent come from an unchurched or dechurched background, so the demand for a very creative, relevant worship experience is extremely high. Rising to the challenge, Mark has become known over the last couple of years as one of the most creative pastors in the country. Recently I was able to ask him about creating a great worship experience.

How important has a great worship experience been in the growth of NCC?

One of the mistakes we made in our church-planting days was marketing NCC. It was a mistake because, honestly, our weekend experience was pretty poor. So we were spending money inviting people to come and see how poorly we do church to ensure they never come back! First things first, you've got to create an experience that is worth inviting friends to. I had a singular goal going into church planting: Create an experience that people felt confident and compelled to invite their friends to! That when they missed church, they actually missed it!

The weekend worship experience is your bread and butter. It will either limit or leverage your influence. Put as much time, energy, and money as possible into it!

What are your criteria for an excellent weekend worship experience?

We have a creative team that meets weekly to plan weekend services. We try to brand all of our sermon series. We produce trailers and invite cards and graphics. And then we add creative elements and worship songs that fit our weekly Big Idea. I think one key is not trying to do too much! Less is more. Each weekend we want to communicate one thing. That's it.

The true criterion for me is 1 Corinthians 14:25: "God is really among you!" I want people to know that they have been in the presence of God. It is tough to measure that, but there are weeks when you know it happened and weeks when you know it didn't. It comes down to this for me: Did we creatively and authentically give people a chance to connect with Christ in a meaningful way this weekend?

How do you deal with volunteers who do not have the gifts or talents to fill a role in your weekend worship experience?

We plug them into small groups. That is a great way for newbies to develop skills. We also have to field four worship teams each weekend for our four locations, and the standard of excellence had to be lowered ever so slightly to accommodate growth. We live in that tension all the time!

Do you think an excellent weekend worship experience should be a priority in a smaller church? Why or why not?

Absolutely. It doesn't matter what size your church is: you've got to give God everything you've got every weekend! Excellence honors God. If you want to experience growth, I think you have to prioritize your weekend service. Think about it in stewardship terms. Let's say one hundred people attend your church and you preach for a half hour. Add it up and that is fifty hours. Who wants to waste fifty hours? You've got to make the most of their time.

What is the first thing you would do if you were pastoring a small church with limited resources to immediately improve the weekend experience?

I would do several things. First, I'd form a creative team. Our first creative team was not paid staff. Just find people who are creative, with an eye for excellence and a heart for God. Begin meeting weekly and start brainstorming sermon series. Not every series has to be off-the-hook creative! Most of them can be peanut butter and jelly. But start by branding a series complete with graphics, videos, and invite cards. Stretch yourself. And then learn from that series and build off of it. Second, I'd set aside a budget for message props and promotions. Spend some money on staging. Or just rearrange the stage. Spend some money on sermon props that will supplement the message. Finally, pray like crazy. No one who walks through our doors is there by accident. They are there by divine appointment. Prayer is free!

IQ Test

Gather a group of leaders together and discuss the following questions. Be sure to include people from your music team and children's ministry, as well as people who simply attend on the weekends rather than lead a ministry.

1. What is the purpose of your Sunday morning service? What are you trying to accomplish?

2. Does God brag about your weekend services to the angels? Why or why not?

3. What do people remember from last weekend's service? What will they remember after this weekend?

4. Review the ten ways to improve your church's worship experience. In which area are you doing the best? In which area does your church need to improve immediately? What is the first step you will take in this area?

5. How do your people experience the power and presence of God in your weekend services? How do your weekend services prepare them to experience God throughout their week?

SETTLING FOR
LOW QUALITY IN
CHILDREN'S MINISTRY

NEXT WEEK:
THE FLANNEL-
GRAPH STORY
OF SISERA!

"IF FLANNELGRAPH BIBLE STORIES WERE GOOD ENOUGH FOR ME,
THEY'RE GOOD ENOUGH FOR YOUR CHILDREN."

I have a confession to make: I grew up hating church. Sunday was always the worst day of the week, except for weeks when I had to go to the dentist. Even then it was a close second. I hated Sunday school, I hated children's church, and I hated children's choir. Sunday school always took place in a dingy little room decorated with pictures of a slightly effeminate Jesus carrying sheep. Not exactly the kind of environment that fires up the imagination of a rowdy group of nine-year-old boys. Every week the teacher, who was no more excited to be there than we were, would put cartoon Bible characters on a flannel board and read from a curriculum that seemed to have been written by a disgruntled spinster. Mercifully the bell would finally ring, releasing all the children from their Sunday school prison cells into the children's church auditorium — a room very similar to the Sunday school classrooms, only larger. In children's church we would sing inane songs with meaningless motions ("Father Abraham had many sons, and many sons had Father Abraham") and listen to improbable stories about children from other countries who had life a lot harder than us. I remember thinking, "At least they don't have to go to church on Sundays." When "big church" would run long, we would play the "Quiet Game," in which the quietest child was selected to come to the front of the auditorium and choose another quiet child to take her place. Even when this game went on forever, I was never chosen. I was finally emancipated from children's church at the age of eleven when the director marched me into big church and asked me never to return. It was an invitation I was more than happy to accept. I hated church and dreamed of the day I could leave and never return.

Somewhere between getting kicked out of children's church and entering Bible college, God changed my mind about church. I never fell in love with the church I attended with my parents, but I knew God was calling me to be a part of a different kind of church in the future. I knew that if a church wanted to impact the next generation, it would have to completely change its approach to children's ministry. To reach children in their formative years, we have to create environments that are geared to today's children and build a curriculum that relates to what they understand and are interested in.

Effective children's ministry has never been more important to the life of the church than it is today. In my generation children went to church because their parents told them to. My parents were not particularly concerned whether I was having a good time at church. When I would ask my mother if I had to go, she would always respond, "No, you *get* to go to church." That dynamic has completely reversed; parents now go to church if their children want to. In a growing congregation, ministry to children cannot be a back-burner issue. Not only do children often determine if and when the family goes to church; the reality is that most people who commit their life to Christ do so before they are eighteen years old. When we focus on the adults and hope for the best for the children, we are missing the major opportunity of the twenty-first-century church.

I did not come to this realization of the importance of children's ministry entirely on my own; I married someone who is passionate about children, all children. Sherry has been a schoolteacher and school administrator. She has run a child development center and sat on the school board of private Christian schools. She currently oversees a school for AIDS orphans in Kenya. In addition, she has worked in children's ministry continuously since age sixteen as an assistant, teacher, department head, and director. Until recently she oversaw the children's ministry at all of Seacoast's campuses. I asked Sherry, based on her own experience, to explain how pastors can build an effective children's ministry in any church.

Starting from Scratch

When Geoff started as pastor at Church on the Lake just outside of Houston, it was a small church with a total child population of two: one older elementary child and one preschool grandchild, who were clearly used to whiling away their mandatory church sentence rolling a Hot Wheels car along the pew, counting the minutes until the last prayer. The first time I saw this, my heart sank. What was their opinion of church? That it was boring and irrelevant? Something to be endured? Exactly.

I had never been asked to start a children's ministry before but had always been fortunate to participate in one that was already there. And while these programs had never been perfect, at least they were *something*. I was starting with *nothing*. Big difference. My background in public school education was both a detriment and a blessing. I understood the way children learn and their developmental needs. But this wasn't school, with homework and report cards and trained teachers earning a salary. This was the place for kids to come to learn about a God who loves them completely, just as they are. A place where they could discover the best friend they'd ever have in their whole lives. A place designed to be, as Sue Miller, former director of children's ministry at Willow Creek Church, says, "the best hour of a child's week."

So where was I to start? I already had some general principles in my head. Children's ministry has to be purposeful. It has to be fun. It has to be organized. But I soon found out I had a lot more to learn. How would I gather my team? What should our goals be, and even harder, how would we know when we had met them? In the next year and a half, as we put together the beginnings of a children's ministry program, I learned a ton, and the more I learned, the more I uncovered that I didn't know. But as my grandpa used to say, "No need to choke a horse with more food than he can chew in one feeding." Let's start with the basics.

What Is Children's Ministry Anyway?

It's easiest to start with what children's ministry is not. It's *not* church for short people. Anybody who has spent time with kids knows that kids like to *do* things. They like to wiggle and talk and laugh and ask questions. They are not horrified by messes and surprises. They like purposeful noise and are drawn to the unexpected. They love bright colors and giggles and don't come with a lot of expectations of what church should be. They love to have fun and, even more, love to love grown-ups who love being around them. So this is where we started, with our target audience: children. I thought about who they were, what they loved, and most important, what they needed. I knew we needed designated spaces for the children to do what they do best: make messes and noise. I found rooms we could set up just for kids. Far enough away from the adult auditorium, but close enough so Mom's heart could still have peace. I knew that all ages don't learn and interact the same, so I started with three areas: babies, preschool, and elementary. We painted. We cleaned. I brought my own two kids into the rooms and asked them, "What would children this age like to play with? What could we put in these rooms that would draw them in and say 'Come in and have fun'?"

I then began to look around for people who seemed to like kids to be on my team — not an easy task. Should I ask the woman who, from the look on her face, had issues with constipation? The guy who came straight from work with a hunting knife strapped to his belt? (What kind of job requires a belt with a hunting knife holder?) While in a sense I felt desperation, I did have some clear answers. The woman who asked if we could just put the kids in a room with crayons and let them "play on their own" was passed over. This was my introduction to lesson number one.

Lesson 1: It Matters Who's on Your Team

We didn't have the hippest church brimming with cool young adults sporting Diesel jeans and funked-out hair. We did, however, have middle-aged blue-collar folks who worked hard, wore sensible shoes, and bought their pants at Kmart. I looked hard at our crowd. Who loved to laugh? Who seemed to have energy? Who had a story of how Jesus had changed their life and had a passion for sharing it? Who could teach a lesson and not make the kids fall over with boredom? I heard Reggie Joiner explain it this way at a recent North

Point Community Church children's conference: "Do not beg people to volunteer in children's ministry. You need to know that your potential team members' need to volunteer is bigger than your need to have a warm body in the room." I chose with care.

So now what? I had a few committed (perhaps coerced) folks who genuinely cared about kids and knew the critical importance of aiming God's love right at them with creativity and excellence. Big deal. What should we *do*? This led me to lesson two.

Lesson 2: It Matters What You Do

Great-looking spaces with fun toys don't equal a quality life-changing program. It's great to look good, but when it comes to children, God expects us to *be* good. Children matter to him, and therefore every element of their program should matter to us. We started with a high-energy curriculum packed with purposeful games and lessons. The curriculum allowed for laughter and movement and surprise, and non-professionally trained teachers could easily understand and invest in it. (At Seacoast we have found 252Basics from the reThinkGroup [www.252Basics.com] to be the most effective curriculum on the market.) Our team members came to understand that children are too important for them to show up unprepared and that 'just winging it' wasn't going to cut it. Each lesson was a chance for life change, and we soon came to realize that the hour on Sunday went by quickly. Wasted time equaled wasted chance and ushered in our worst enemies: boredom and its ugly stepsister, discipline problems.

We learned to program every moment with purposeful dialogue, engaging Bible stories, and relevant activities. We reminded ourselves often that we weren't dealing with a room full of height-challenged idiots who didn't know the difference between an engaging game with purpose and a coloring sheet. Quality mattered. Children are intelligent and discerning, and they know what they like. As time went on, we began to realize that each phase of the schedule was important and to prepare for the two questions that would be asked of the children — not by us, but by their parents at pick-up time. This discovery led to my third lesson.

Lesson 3: It Matters What the Parents Think

One of my favorite things to do in the churches where I've been on staff is to poke around outside the children's department during dismissal time. Moms and dads wait expectantly in line to pick up their darlings. The children fly out of their rooms with papers and crafts in hand, and the first "high holy" question is put forth: "Did you have fun?" And then the second question: "What did you do?" I have to admit the answers to these questions carry much more weight with the parents than I gave them credit for in my early years of children's ministry. If the child mumbles, "No" and "Nothin'," we are in trouble. I can see the look of concern on Mom's face. She is thinking, "You didn't like it? Well, I'm not going to bring my little genius back to something she didn't *like*!" I have learned the importance of bright faces emerging from the children's rooms, accompanied by bouncy steps and excited voices not waiting for the sacred questions but rather interrupting with, "You're not gonna believe what we did today!" This is not only the reaction parents are looking for, but the one they rely on. Agree with it or not, we are living in a culture where families are incredibly child-centered. Is it reasonable that parents should make their child's satisfaction with the children's ministry the sole determining factor of whether they will go to your church? No. Is it a reality? Yes.

The bigger issue, however, is that we need the parents on our side. Parents are the number one spiritual leaders in their children's lives. It is our job to partner with them, gain their confidence, and arm them with the tools to lead their children in their relationship with Christ. We only have the children for one hour on Sunday; their parents have them for the rest of the week. The best we can hope for is to reinforce what the children are already learning at home. Reggie

Joiner recently challenged children's leaders with this question: "What would happen if you started acting like what happens at home might be more important than what happens at church?"

I learned the hard way that we can't facilitate Christian learning at home if our children's ministry stinks. And I've discovered that the last fifteen minutes of our time each Sunday are the most important minutes we have. We can't let the program peter out while we are waiting for "big church" to let out. We have to reinforce our main lesson point in a fun way so our precious little geniuses can answer their parents' two questions that we know are coming. And we need to make our take-home papers sharp, aimed at "family" and not just child. We have to give parents all the tools they need.

After a couple of years at Church on the Lake, we moved to Seacoast, which is located in a completely different type of town. Instead of mainly blue-collar workers, the population is mostly professional, with middle to upper incomes. Lots of stay-at-home moms with custom-designed nurseries and children's bedrooms complete with the latest toys and electronic gadgets. That's when I was faced with lesson four.

Lesson 4: It Matters That You Know What Your Families Expect

I can feel you bristling. Maybe you're thinking, "Are you suggesting that we tailor our programs based on our families' financial status? That only wealthy children matter?" No, all children matter. But I am suggesting that you know your audience and anticipate their expectations. At Seacoast I learned quickly that our nurseries have to be not only safe and secure, but also supplied with the latest in baby-care accoutrements. At Church on the Lake, our nursery had to be clean; at Seacoast, our nurseries have to be hypoallergenic. Our preschoolers and elementary students are accustomed to the latest in media entertainment, so we need to keep one step ahead of them in our children's programming. While the safety and quality of our program were just as important to parents at our previous church, the families at Seacoast are inspecting us to see if we know what they are about and what they are used to. They expect us to pay attention to current trends in child care, education, and decor and follow suit. I quickly learned to ask questions about the things I knew the parents weren't telling me but were talking to each other about. And I learned to listen.

Where Do We Get Started?

If you want to ensure you have a dynamic, life-changing children's ministry, I (Geoff) suggest you start where Sherry finished and learn to listen. Ask individual parents what they think about the children's ministry. What do their children like the most? What areas need to improve? Ask your children's workers if they have everything they need to be effective. If nothing was impossible, what would they add to your current children's ministry?

Next, begin to dream together with your children's teams. Visit other churches with dynamic children's ministries and dream together. For children's ministry workers, nothing is more invigorating than knowing that their pastor is fully engaged in what they are trying to accomplish. Take a weekend off from preaching and volunteer in the nursery and in the other departments. Formulate a plan for how you can radically improve the way your church reaches out to the next generation.

When you have a plan for the new look and feel of the children's ministry, build it into the budget. Make sure the children's ministry gets the piece of the pie it needs and deserves. Since more than 85 percent of people who commit their lives to Christ do so as children and children are determining the church attendance of the entire family, the children's department should get a lion's share of the total budget.

Finally, begin to champion children's ministry from the pulpit. Don't beg for volunteers; coerced volunteers usually last a short time and are almost always ineffective. Instead, weave life-change stories through your sermons. Talk about children who are giving their lives to Christ, volunteers who are finding fulfillment through ministering to kids, and positive experiences you have had working in the children's ministry. Never make working with children sound like punishment. Celebrate the fun and life change that happen just a few yards down the hall every weekend. When you go public with your commitment to children's ministry, parents will know that you care about what they care about and volunteers will be inspired to get involved. And children's lives will be changed for eternity.

With six children of his own, Craig Groeschel is deeply invested in the children's ministry of the church he planted, LifeChurch.tv, based in Edmond, Oklahoma. His passion comes through loud and clear in our discussion of the importance of a quality children's ministry in a growing church.

····················· **SPOTLIGHT**··················
Craig Groeschel, LifeChurch.tv

When I met LifeChurch.tv's (www.lifechurch.tv) leadership team at a Leadership Network event, my first thought was, "Who are these crazy guys from Oklahoma?" At the time they had about seven thousand people attending four campuses, but their vision was to open dozens of campuses all over America and beyond. They talked in terms of tens of thousands of attendees and dreamed of changing the world. Five years later they now have campuses in Oklahoma, Arizona, Texas, Tennessee, New York, and Florida, as well as an Internet campus with more than twenty thousand people attending a LifeChurch.tv experience every weekend.

One of the things I've been most impressed with at LifeChurch.tv is the leaders' unwavering commitment to quality ministry to children. Whenever they talk about core values, they go back to the vital importance of children in the mission God has given them. And this unswerving dedication to reaching the next generation comes directly from the founding pastor at LifeChurch, Craig Groeschel. I recently had the opportunity to ask Craig about this dedication and why it is important to every church.

How important is children's ministry in the life of a church? Why?

One of the most fulfilling aspects of being a part of a church like LifeChurch.tv is seeing people become followers of Christ. Jesus offered us the analogy of "fishing for men." We can picture ourselves casting with a rod and reel, bringing people in one by one. But the kind of fishing that Jesus' disciples would have been familiar with was nothing like that. They used nets. The real net-bursting opportunities for changed lives — lives that represent the future of the church globally — are down the hall, in the brightly painted, brightly lit rooms of LifeKIDS. If you don't plan generationally in your ministry, your church will age with you. And it will die right along with you too. It would be easy for me as a pastor to focus on my own demographic, ministering to "me" out there.

Our LifeKIDS staff has made no secret that they're glad Amy and I have six kids. Many of our key leaders also have young children (and even grandchildren). This perspective has always been an important factor in how we relate to families, parents, and kids. Of course, you don't have to be a parent to lead a growing church. But you can't welcome families and minister to them with authenticity if you ignore their realities.

How do you emphasize children's ministry in your church?

You can walk into any church and know within a few minutes where the kids rank. Do the color scheme and architecture target adults? Children? Both? Be honest. When you walk into a LifeChurch.tv campus, you can tell right away that much of the design is tailored to appeal to kids. Giant elephant cutouts, colorful bright signs, and friendly cartoon characters point the way to the action.

Put your money where your mouth is. Matthew 6:21 promises that's where your heart will be. Budgeting for children's ministry is not an afterthought. Church budgets vary widely, but you can't expect your church to really thrive if you don't factor kids into your decisions. We've invested in making parents feel safe about leaving their kids in our care, and we show kids of all ages that church is the place to be. We want them there. And they know it. They can see it.

What are the key elements of an excellent children's ministry? What are you looking for?

This is typically a challenging question for a senior pastor. We think that's why we have children's pastors — to rattle off answers like that so we don't have to! But the truth is, every person in your leadership should know this one. Of course, you should delegate the authority and tasks of children's ministry to those who are called to lead it. But all leadership must take an active interest and participate in this incredibly important area. Children's ministry isn't a separate department. It's a strategic component of the ministry as a whole — only shorter.

The key elements of an excellent children's ministry are solid safety procedures, an environment that is comfortable and aesthetically pleasing to a child, great curriculum that teaches biblical truth and how to apply it, and most importantly, an amazing team of volunteer leaders who understand the vision of your ministry.

Now, I don't need to know what characters are on screen or what units they're doing this week. But I should always be able to answer these three questions:

1. Is it effective?

2. Is it aligned with the church's vision?

3. Is it being led with purpose?

LifeKIDS' ministry is effectively producing spiritual growth in our children. The way it functions is strategically aligned with the ministry model of our church. And LifeKIDS is being intentionally directed and coordinated to accomplish its stated, agreed-to mission. At our church, senior leadership provides this direction, and we evaluate all three criteria regularly.

How do you resource children's ministry at your church? How does it compare to other ministries as a percentage of your overall ministry budget?

One of LifeChurch.tv's core values is stewardship. Because of that — and not in spite of it — we spend a *lot* of money on kids. Because God led us to create our own curriculum, rather than just purchasing some off the shelf, our production costs are high. Our multicampus model allows us to get a lot of mileage from this expense already. However, all of our LifeKIDS curriculum, including videos, lesson plans, and all other materials, are now poised to be shared on our OPEN website (www.open.lifechurch.tv). When you calculate this kind of potential ROI, the value is well worth the cost.

Another area where we don't skimp is what LifeKIDS' environments look like. Although the murals, lights, and noise may not directly change lives, they make kids feel welcome, and they want to come back and bring their friends. One of our LifeKIDS staff members told us this true story a few years ago: A family was visiting LifeChurch.tv for the first time on Easter. Their older elementary–aged boy froze when he walked into the lobby, and he shouted, "You call this a *church*?" And that's exactly the kind of reaction we want. We're not in competition with the church down the street. Culturally, we're going head-to-head with Disney.

Because of our investment in quality children's ministry, kids fifth grade and under represent over a fifth of most campuses' attendance. If you include parents and volunteers, that's a huge chunk of our body being ministered to. Also, in a typical week, LifeKIDS has several more experiences per week than "big church." When I preach one time, that may represent twelve different campuses, but during that same hour, LifeKIDS will have anywhere from four to eleven separate experiences — per campus — running at the same time. Looking at it that way, the budget percentage is clearly appropriate. So considering the scope and scale of the ministry that LifeKIDS executes each week, it really doesn't matter how it compares to other ministry departments or programs. That's an apples-to-oranges comparison.

What immediate steps would you take if you were pastoring a small church with limited resources to improve your children's ministry?

The responsibility of leading children to become fully devoted followers of Christ is one of the most daunting tasks you can face. It's an intimidating challenge for even the most spiritually grounded. Here's what we believe (because it's scriptural): God has placed that task squarely on the shoulders of parents. So our role is to offer them a support system. Our mission for LifeKIDS is to partner with parents to provide the skills, experiences, and resources that will enable their children to become fully devoted followers of Christ. Skills, experiences, and resources. As the church, our staff, volunteers, and curriculum can offer these three things in a way that parents may not have the means to provide — an exciting weekend experience, a tight relationship with a group of Christian peers, an adult leader who is speaking the same truths into their lives that parents are, service and leadership opportunities, take-home materials that equip parents to continue the teaching they get at church — the possibilities are endless. The best steps you can take become simple when you start with that in mind.

1. *Begin and end every planning session with how the program assists parents.* That does not mean the babysitting mentality: "We need someone to watch the kids so we 'real Christians' can meet." That does mean you have to incorporate some kind of communication feature that informs parents of what the kids are learning and how they can continue the lesson at home. We get them for a couple of hours a week if we're lucky. Mom and Dad get the rest of the week. If we can leverage our influence into those hours, we'll clearly have a much greater impact. Focusing on keeping parents in the driver's seat is crucial.

2. *Choose curriculum that aligns with your church mission and discipleship process.* For example, we offer weekend experiences for adults that are designed to be comfortable for guests while being confrontational about sin. For deeper growth, we ask them to be a part of a LifeGroup. In the same way, LifeKIDS offers weekend experiences that don't make kids feel like the new kid in class. If they drop in any week, they'll have a great time and learn about Jesus. For further growth, we offer elementary kids KONNECT. This small group experience meets one evening a week for two hours, so parents can attend LifeGroups during that same time. Although we create our own curriculum to get a perfect match, many great curriculum series are available to purchase — as long as you carefully review them with alignment in mind. Remember: you can't judge a book by its cover.

3. *Don't confuse entertainment (or very structured curriculum) with true engagement.* In many cases, parents have perceived the beige walls and workbooks of their children's church as a sign of real learning. On the other hand, some families have been a part of children's ministry that seems very entertaining. In either case, neither entertainment nor

curriculum alone equals true engagement. We've learned that providing an environment that draws kids, coupled with programming that leads kids to biblical truth and how to apply it, is the best combination. Engage focus groups of kids and parents and get some educators or other experts in your church to help you assess the effectiveness of your ministry over time. You should have clearly stated outcomes, and you should check regularly to see how you're doing.

4. *Do what you can, when you can.* LifeKIDS didn't start its first day with slides and talking trees. Each LifeChurch.tv campus starts with a package of features appropriate for the size and budget of the campus. We refer to it as "right-sizing." As a campus grows, we add additional experiences, decorative themes, staff, and other materials — but only as a campus can afford those things. You can't buy church growth. (We've learned that the hard way ... more than once.) But don't just throw your hands up and quit because you don't have the resources. Make a plan and do something, even if it's just painting your halls bright colors. Paint's not expensive. Do *something*.

IQ Test

Gather a group of children's leaders and discuss the following questions. Be sure to have someone take notes on the answers you arrive at. Next, gather a group of parents and ask the same questions, again taking notes. Finally, get together with your children's leaders again. Write the answers they gave on a poster board and the answers the parents gave on another poster board and discuss the gaps. Come up with an action plan together to reframe your children's ministry.

1. What is the purpose of our children's ministry?
2. Where is our children's ministry strongest? Where is it weakest?

3. How are we partnering with parents in the spiritual formation of their children? How could we be more intentional about doing so?

4. If money were no object, what are the first three things we would do to improve our children's ministry? How can we begin implementing these ideas within our present budget?

5. How can we measure the ongoing effectiveness of our children's ministry?

5

PROMOTING TALENT
OVER INTEGRITY

"WE KNOW HE'S A THIEF AND A LIAR,
BUT NO ONE CAN MAKE THE ORGAN SING LIKE BOB."

One day John (all names in this chapter have been changed to protect everyone involved) just showed up. No one knew exactly how he'd come to our church, but no one looked too closely; you see, John was an incredibly talented young man with just the gifts we needed. He was an amazing guitar player and a magnetic worship leader. Everywhere John went he attracted a group of followers. Within a few weeks of his first visit, John was leading a small group of teenagers and volunteering on our worship team. Before long John was one of the leaders of our student ministry and helped lead our weekend worship service. John seemed to be a true gift from God with a bright future — a real answer to prayer.

There were some challenges. Some of our leaders had an uneasy feeling about John; they couldn't put their finger on it, but something didn't seem quite right. Maybe it was John's stories. Although he was young, he told stories of leading worship all over the world and meeting many well-known Christian leaders. These stories were always interesting and funny, but it was hard to fit all of John's experiences into the short timeline of his life. Maybe the uneasiness came from John's sense of humor. His personal stories were often borderline tasteless and tinged with a hint of perversion that made his audience squirm. We began to check a little closer into John's background but didn't find any red flags; there were cracks in his character, but nothing we couldn't deal with. If John had been less talented or less willing to serve, we might have been more cautious, but by this time he was invaluable to what we were trying to accomplish.

Then one day the dam broke. A teenager in John's small group came to one of our leaders and told him that John had engaged in some very inappropriate behavior. The leader confronted John about the accusation, but John denied it. The leader began to call other teenagers in the group, and one by one the stories began to come out. It soon became apparent that John was a very sick young man. We called John in and gave him another chance to confess, but again he denied everything. With very heavy hearts we told John that his time at the church was over and that he faced a very difficult future.

We prayed for John and then escorted him from the building. Later that day the police arrested John, and he eventually pled guilty to several charges and was placed on probation. We have met with John on several occasions since that day, but he continues to struggle with facing the truth about his past and finding healing for his future. Although John has walked away from any accountability program, he continues to find churches where he can sing and play, because John is a talented young man with just the gifts they need.

This story is one I hear repeated over and over as I talk to pastors. It isn't about doing background checks or checking references; we did all of that with John, and the results came back clean. Those are the easy, basic steps we should take with any leader. The bigger questions are these: Why do we promote talent over integrity? How do we detect when there might be an integrity problem? What do we do when we discover that a leader has integrity issues? Let's tackle these questions one at a time.

Why Are We Suckers for Talent?

Before you get too self-righteous about the story I just told, put yourself in our place. An incredibly talented, bright, seemingly spiritually mature young man just walks into your church out of the blue. He has tons of experience, seems to fit into your culture, and wants to work massive hours for free. You would jump at the chance — you know you would.

Talent that walks in off the street is much quicker and easier to deploy than talent you have to develop. That's why the New York Yankees are willing to spend millions of dollars a year for someone like Alex Rodriguez; they get instant bang for their buck. It can take years to develop a worship leader, a youth pastor, a small group director. If you can just grab one ready-made off the rack, you can accomplish so much more immediately. We use microwaves for our food, superfast computers for our work and play, and instant messaging for our communication; why wouldn't we want to speed up our leadership development with talent right out of the box?

And let's not forget the wow factor of instant talent. Everything else just seems better when you have a great musician, singer, or artist involved in your weekend service. It's easier to preach a great sermon after an amazing guitar solo, breathtaking vocals, and a video that brings tears to your eyes. You need eye-popping talent to pull off that level of excellence; when you find individuals with that kind of talent, you want to hold on to them. It's also rare to find a children's ministry leader who can keep the attention of children who are inundated every day with the Disney Channel, Nickelodeon, and PlayStation 3; when you find one, it's easy to overlook a few flaws along the way.

And talent attracts talent. Early on at Seacoast we had a hard time finding good guitar players. Our music is normally very contemporary and therefore very guitar driven. We had great keyboard players, great drummers, even a world-class saxophonist, but we could only find mediocre (at best) guitar players. After we had prayed many months for a guitar player, Keith showed up. Keith was a monster player who blew away everyone else on stage. Suddenly guitar players began coming out of the woodwork. Some were friends of Keith, some knew him by reputation, some were simply attracted when they visited Seacoast and heard him play. We now have several amazing guitar players (including Keith) all because one very talented musician showed up and started playing. Talent is a good thing and a gift from God; the problem is when we let talent trump integrity.

How Do I Know If a Talented Leader Has Integrity?
Check the Dental Work

The first key to detecting integrity is to look a gift horse in the mouth. When anything in life seems too good to be true, it usually is; as a pastor, I'm responsible for finding the warts. Every talented individual who walks in off the street and volunteers for ministry came from somewhere. Where have they served in the past? Why did they leave? Did they leave on good terms? A call to their former pastor is always in order, and it's always a good idea to dig beneath the surface and ask the uncomfortable questions. "What are you not telling me about John? Do you have any misgivings about his character?" God has called us to protect the flock, and that begins with some difficult conversations with other shepherds in the field.

Take the Duck Test

A second key is what I call the duck test. There is a great scene in the movie *Monty Python and the Holy Grail* in which a group of peasants is trying to determine if a local girl is really a witch. When one of King Arthur's knights who is traveling through the village asks the peasants why they think she is a witch, one of the villagers exclaims, "She looks like one." (Another peasant has put a witch's hat on her and attached a carrot to her nose.) The knight then leads them through a bewildering exercise in twisted logic, beginning with the fact that witches are made of wood and ending with this seemingly irrefutable maxim: "If she weighs the same as a duck, she's a witch!" The villagers then determine the fate of the young girl by putting her on a scale with a duck. I don't want to spoil the suspense, but it does not end well for the fair maiden.

The point is this: when assessing talented individuals (or any leader in the church), we need to ask, "Does this person pass the duck test?" If it walks like a duck, quacks like a duck, and weighs the same as a duck, it is probably a duck. What are the facts about the individual in question? Are there unsettling details that could point to an uncomfortable conclusion? Do their stories not always seem to add up? Do their finances seem out of control? Is their time sometimes difficult to account for? Do they seem to be a little too friendly with the opposite sex? Do they frequently tell stories that make the people around them uneasy? We should avoid incessant witch hunts, but we should also listen to our instincts and the instincts of the leaders around us. If there are persistent, nagging questions about an individual, we need to consider that we may be dealing with a duck.

Put Courtship before Marriage

A third key in integrity detection is to be sure to date before you marry. My wife and I dated for five years before we got married, so we knew each other very well before we finally walked down the aisle. (I tried to get her to marry me sooner, but she was only fifteen when we started dating.) Over the past twenty-six years of marriage, we've had our ups and downs and have each grown in different ways, but we've had no big surprises.

When you are considering deploying new leaders, spend time getting to know them before putting them in a position of influence. You need an opportunity to observe them in a variety of circumstances to see how they react. Your other leaders need the chance to get to know them up close before being linked with them in a ministry partnership. The best practice is to ask them to attend your church for at least six months before they take on any leadership role. They can spend time getting to know the rhythm of your ministry, the discipleship process at your church, and the leadership structure already in place. During that time you can connect with them as well as your key leaders and determine whether you should put them on the duck scale. The nice thing about dating is that you can always break up; once you're married, things get much more complicated.

Listen to the Critics

A fourth key to discovering lapses in integrity is to listen to the critics. This step is a hard one for me; I don't like critics. I want everyone to be on the bandwagon leading the cheers and extolling the greatness of our ministry. I get irritated when I hear that the music is too loud, the message is too long, and the air-conditioning is too cold. I tend to throw the labels Sanballat and Tobiah (Nehemiah 2, 4, 6) around too freely and quickly dismiss critics. We do have to guard against dwelling on criticism, or we will wind up depressed and unable to do what God created us to do. The reality, however, is that sometimes the critics have valid points. Sometimes the hypersensitive types will be the first to detect a fault in the character of a leader. We shouldn't let critics assassinate our leaders, but we do need to listen when we hear similar complaints from more than one person. Where there's smoke, there may not be fire, but there's probably some kind of spark.

I was on staff many years ago at a growing church in Texas. Contemporary worship was just beginning to influence churches, and we had one of the most talented worship leaders in the country. He had an amazing voice, a real feel for what music would connect with our congregation, and he was a magnet for other talented singers and musicians. We were gaining a reputation as *the* place to be if you wanted to experience this new wave of worship in our city. In the midst of all the excitement, we also had our critics. Along with the complaints about the drums, the guitar, and the volume, we heard hints that our worship leader was very egocentric. People were concerned that our worship was more about the leader than about God. There were also concerns about his appearance and his "comfort" around the opposite sex. It was easy to dismiss the criticism because the services were going superbly and people's lives were being changed as the church continued to grow.

And then one day the wheels came off. One of the musicians came to our senior pastor and said that he had caught his wife in an affair with the worship pastor. When the worship pastor was confronted, he admitted the affair and resigned his position. The damage he'd done, however, had just begun. The more we looked, the more garbage we found. The lack of integrity of one man eventually led to the erosion of the entire ministry of that church. Today only a handful of people are left in the congregation.

It pays to keep a positive attitude, to refuse to give in to Sanballat and Tobiah, and, at the same time, to investigate critics' charges thoroughly. It's a lot easier to snuff out a spark than to extinguish a raging wildfire. We have watched recently as prominent churches have been destroyed because no one paid attention to the critics who said there was a flaw in the integrity of key leaders.

Ask the Tough Questions

The final key to detecting a lack of integrity is to ask the hard questions. These conversations are never fun, but they are absolutely necessary to the life of the church and the growth of leaders. I'll never forget meeting Brian, one of our children's ministry leaders, at my favorite little Mexican restaurant. (I always figure the food might as well be good even if the conversation is tough.) Brian had a huge heart for ministry. Once while driving a back road in South Carolina, Brian hit a deer. He was okay and his truck wasn't damaged, but he felt terrible. He couldn't imagine just leaving the deer carcass beside the road to rot, so he threw it into the back of his truck. He wasn't a hunter and had no idea what he'd do with the deer until he remembered an orphanage he had read about in the newspaper. On a whim he drove straight to the orphanage, and asked if they could use a freshly killed deer. The cook was thrilled and immediately took the deer. When Brian saw the conditions the children faced at the orphanage he knew he had to do something, so he gathered some friends and started an outreach ministry to the children living there. Every week they would go to the orphanage, teach a Bible study, and hang out with the children. On Sundays they would borrow a church van and bring the kids to Seacoast. Brian and his friends then began volunteering in children's ministry because the children they were bringing were more than our staff could handle.

Brian was a high-capacity volunteer. He not only worked in the ministry; he recruited, inspired, and trained other volunteers. He was the kind of guy you gave plaques to, not someone you called on the carpet. But something wasn't quite right. There were gaps in Brian's story, rumors that his lifestyle didn't live up to his testimony. So over quesadillas and Diet Coke, I presented Brian with what I had heard. He was shocked, dismayed, couldn't believe what I was saying. He was offended, hurt, and disappointed, and he denied everything. My gut reaction was that Brian was covering up something very dark inside, but we continued to try to work with him. It became more and more obvious, however, that something just wasn't right. Eventually we had to ask Brian to step down from ministry.

Over time we came to realize that Brian had serious psychological problems that he was able to mask with frantic activity and hyper-commitment to a cause. His desire to serve came from something unhealthy deep inside himself. While we were able to protect the children from any harm, we weren't able to rescue Brian. His life continued to unravel over time and ended tragically a couple of years ago.

If your church contains any Brians — hypercommitted, very talented volunteers — don't hesitate to ask the hard questions. If their lives seem out of balance, ask them to give an accounting of their time. If they seem to exhibit an unusual attraction to the opposite (or same) sex, ask them about their intimate life. If they have gaps in their schedule that are hard to explain, ask them to tell you where they've been. If they seem on top of the mountain part of the time and in the depths of the valley at others, explore that tendency with them as well. When at all possible, have at least one or two others with you for these conversations, and listen with your heart and your head. Ask God to give you discernment, and go beyond what you want to hear to find out the truth. If you are still uneasy after one of these encounters, God is probably revealing something that will have to be dealt with.

How Do We Recover from a Lapse of Integrity?

So how do we deal with volunteers or staff members in whom we discover an integrity issue? The first response is to kick them out. Isn't that what Paul meant when he told the Corinthians, "You should remove this man from your fellowship" (1 Cor. 5:2 NLT)? Later in the same chapter he says, "You must remove the evil person from among you" (v. 13 NLT). I certainly agree that if you discover that one of your key leaders is sleeping with his stepmother, he needs to go. That's just disgusting. Most integrity challenges, however, come short of incest, so let's look at practical steps we can take before we give the offender the right foot of fellowship.

Discover the Real Issue

The first thing we have to assess is the real issue behind the lapse of integrity. Was this a mistake or an addiction, an error in judgment or a character flaw? A few years ago one of our young leaders, we'll call him Pete, came forward to confess a major mistake in his life; he had failed morally and now a baby was going to be born "prematurely." Pete served in a very public capacity, and everyone who knew him and his girlfriend would have little trouble doing the math and solving the equation. The situation soon became a very public lapse of integrity on the part of a very talented leader. We had known Pete since he had committed his life to Christ a few years before and had watched him grow in his faith as he was discipled by other more mature leaders. This lapse did not characterize Pete, he had come forward on his own, and he was very repentant of both his sin and the impact it might have on the ministry of God through Seacoast Church. We knew that restoration was the right course of action, and today Pete is a vital part of our church. We'll talk more about the restoration process below.

In contrast to Pete's story is the story of my friend Dave. Dave and I connected the first time we met. We had similar backgrounds and the same warped sense of humor, and we both had a passion for ministry. Dave was one of the most talented people I have ever met. He was a brilliant singer and a gifted musician. He was a magnet for children and could build almost anything. When I pastored the little church in Texas, Dave would lead worship during the Sunday service and then hurry over to the children's auditorium to teach the kids. He would come almost every day during the week to build, paint, repair, or clean. On Wednesday night he would lead a group of boys in a program similar to Boy Scouts at the church. Most Saturdays he would spend the whole day helping with whatever needed to be done to prepare for Sunday.

Dave's problem was that he couldn't control his impulses. When he saw something he wanted, he bought it. When he couldn't make the payments, he walked away. I helped Dave move out of several apartments that he was evicted from and a house he lost in a bankruptcy settlement. I kept thinking Dave would change. Each time he got into trouble, I was there for him. I helped him move, I talked his wife into not leaving him, and I talked with his in-laws about not throwing him out. I helped him find a counselor and visited him in the hospital as he battled his inner demons. But Dave never got better. In fact, I suspect that as the years went on, a lot more was going on under the surface than I ever found out about. I loved Dave, but I finally had to walk away. Dave did not have a lapse of integrity or an occasional slip; Dave had a character flaw that led to destructive behavior again and again. I've heard in the last few years that Dave has finally found solid ground and is making a sustained run at living a life of integrity; I often think of him and his exceptional talent and wonder what might have been.

Are you dealing with a Pete in your church or a Dave? Does the integrity issue characterize your leader, or does it seem way out in left field? Is it a first, second, or third offense, or is it a habitual problem? If you have a Pete, let's look at what's next for him. If you have a Dave, we'll discuss how to deal with him at the end of this chapter.

Enforce a Time-Out

The first step in dealing with leaders who have had a lapse of integrity is to have them take a time-out. It's a time in which they can grow in their personal walk with Jesus without the pressure of ministry. It is also a time for them to reflect on what led to the lapse of integrity and to work to build safeguards against a repeat of past behavior. Finally, it is a clear sign to the congregation that we take character and integrity very seriously, and no matter how talented certain individuals may be, they are subject to the same biblical standards as everyone else.

I am concerned when I hear of public Christian leaders who have fallen and, after a brief time away from ministry, are "healed" and ready to get right back into full-time ministry. I wonder how much of their healing has to do with the need or desire to keep the offerings flowing to sustain the megaministry they have built. Anyone in leadership in the church needs a significant time away to allow the Lord to restore what the locusts have eaten. In some cases we have asked people to step away for six months, but usually we ask that they refrain from leading in the church for a period of one year.

The leader's response to being asked to step down will tell a great deal about the condition of his or her heart. When we told Pete that he would have to step away from any public ministry for a significant period of time, he was heartbroken; God had gifted him to lead from the stage, and it was what he lived for. Pete knew, however, that he needed the time away from ministry to heal and to grow, so he submitted to the plan that we laid out and served faithfully behind the scenes for several months. His attitude along with the time away made Pete stronger as a leader when he returned to public ministry several months later.

I had a very different reaction when I sat down with Susan and her direct supervisor to talk about her future in children's ministry. Susan was another one of those super-volunteers. She served every weekend and most Wednesdays in a variety of capacities in our children's ministry. She sang, she taught, and she led a girls' small group. (My daughter was a part of her small group and loved her.) We became concerned when Susan told another volunteer that she could not live without children's ministry. We love commitment, but that comment sounded over the top. Other cracks were appearing in Susan's character as well. When we told Susan we felt she needed to step away from ministry for a while, she went ballistic. How could we put her in time-out? After all she had done for Seacoast and all the time she had poured into the ministry, how dare we tell her she had to "sit down"? I have never faced so much venom in my life. Susan never returned to the children's ministry and eventually left Seacoast. She drifted from church to church and eventually fell into a very destructive lifestyle of drugs and serial relationships. After several years I received a long letter from Susan expressing her regret for her reaction that day and all the hurt she had caused. She said she had finally found peace with God and was working to rebuild her life. My prayer is that Susan will someday fulfill the potential God has placed within her.

Build Accountability

Sometime between Baby Einstein and Algebra II, every child learns the phrase, "I can do it myself." I was introduced to this expression when my son was about three years old. It was my turn to take him to the babysitter on my way to work, and we were running late. Rushing out the door, I realized his shoelaces weren't tied, so I quickly stooped down to tie them. This was a mistake. In tying his shoes I was challenging his intelligence, his athletic ability, and his independence. He had studied the art of intertwining shoelaces and now considered himself an expert in the field. With righteous indignation he exclaimed, "No, Daddy! I can do it myself!" Choosing not to die on this particular hill, I stepped away and let him demonstrate his newly acquired knot skills. We were very, very late that morning.

This urge to "do it myself" stays with us all of our lives. Regardless of the odds, we all have an inner voice that says, "I can do this. I don't need anyone's help." This tendency becomes a major challenge when trying to restore a staff member or volunteer who has struggled with integrity issues. Recently the papers ran a story about a nationally known pastor who had stepped down from leadership because of a moral failure in his life. After a relatively short time-out in his life, he now has declared himself ready to pick up where he left off; he no longer has any need for the accountability group he has been meeting with. He can do it himself.

The reality is that none of us can do it ourselves. We all need ongoing accountability to overcome issues of character and integrity in our lives. When we restore someone to a place of leadership after a lapse, it is vital that we build accountability into that relationship. Who are they meeting with? Are they answering the tough questions?

What safeguards have they instituted in their lives to ensure their future success? Someone who is willing to be held accountable on an ongoing basis is ready to return to ministry. Someone who walks away from accountability isn't. The best thing you can do for your church at that point is to end the relationship.

Know When to Run

In dealing with integrity issues, you have to make sure there is an end to the process. Either the individuals in question are restored to ministry, or they are asked to leave. Several years ago we had to end a relationship with a talented volunteer on our worship team. He was a great guy who had committed his life to Christ at Seacoast and poured himself into every aspect of ministry. On several occasions, however, he was discovered to have had a lapse of judgment. Each time he was confronted, he confessed, took a time-out from ministry, and connected with an accountability partner. After a period of time, he was restored to ministry and the cycle began again. Eventually we had to ask him to step out of ministry entirely. Because of his talent, other churches quickly opened up ministry opportunities, and the cycle continues today. In the words of the famous theologian Kenny Rogers, "You've got to know when to when to walk away, know when to run."

I have a great deal of respect for Dave Ferguson, founding pastor of Community Christian Church based in Naperville, Illinois. Every weekend the church employs talented ministry volunteers at all eight of its campuses located around Chicagoland without compromising on integrity. I asked Dave how his church strikes this balance.

· · · · · · · · · · · · · · · · · · **SPOTLIGHT** · · · · · · · · · · · · · · · ·

Dave Ferguson, Community Christian Church

Dave Ferguson (www.daveferguson.org) is a remarkable thinker and communicator, a point that was driven home for me

by an anonymous comment we received after doing a conference breakout session together with another friend a couple of
years ago: "Let me be blunt. Dave is so much more engaging
than these other two guys that you just wanted to hear what he
had to say and tell the other guys to put a sock in it. It's not that
the other guys weren't worth hearing, but it's evident when you
have a heavyweight and two lighter weights on the stage, and
you're trying to play them off as equals — it just doesn't work
that well."

I wanted to be hurt and offended, but in my case I had to
agree with the comment. When it comes to innovative solutions
for helping people find their way back to God, Dave Ferguson
is definitely a heavyweight. Between the pioneering work he
has done at Community Christian Church (www.communitychris-
tian.org) based in Naperville, Illinois, his book *The Big Idea*
(Zondervan), and the New Thing Network (www.newthing.org)
of reproducing churches, Dave is having a huge impact on the
landscape of the church in North America.

Dave, along with his brother Jon and a team of friends,
started Community Christian Church in 1989 in a growing suburb just outside of Chicago. By 2008 Community Christian had
grown to more than four thousand weekend attendees on eight
campuses spread across the Chicagoland area, in addition to
planting churches across the country. The church has been included on lists of the most innovative, most influential, and fastest-
growing churches in America. It also has helped hundreds of
churches across the country launch multisite ministries through its
hands-on practicums and conferences.

In such a fast-growing, far-flung environment as Community
Christian Church, I know the demand for highly skilled staff and
volunteers can blur the lines between talent with integrity and
talent without integrity. I also know Dave to be an exceptionally
honest and humble leader, so I asked him how the leaders walk
that tightrope at Community Christian.

Have you ever struggled with a talented volunteer or staff member who displayed a lack of character? How did you deal with the situation?

Unfortunately, this is not an unusual situation. The most recent case was with a very talented volunteer leader. When the case was brought to my attention, we tried to follow a three-step process we get from Matthew 18.

> *Step 1*: Go to the person one-on-one in love with the hope that they will respond with repentance and reconciliation.
>
> *Step 2*: If the person doesn't respond with repentance and willingness to reconcile, then go to the person and bring another person with you.
>
> *Step 3*: If the person doesn't respond with repentance and willingness to reconcile, then remove the expectations and the privilege of leadership.

In this case, the first person to go to this leader was the director of the ministry in which he served. When we didn't get a repentant response, the campus pastor went with the ministry director to meet with this person. In this situation the person did repent but was unwilling to reconcile and left the church. I don't consider that a success.

How do you assess the integrity of a potential key volunteer or staff member?

There is both an initial assessment and an ongoing assessment.

Initial assessment. The first assessment of every leader comes as they work through our Leadership Expectations. The Leadership Expectations address a variety of important factors, from a person's belief in Jesus to stewardship, significant relationships, and more. The goal is that every leader understands that these are the expectations for what it means to be a leader at Community Christian Church. Some of the questions we ask all of our new leaders include the following:

1. What have you been talking to God about lately? What has he been saying in return?

2. How are you growing in relationship with God through participation in Celebration Services?

3. How are you experiencing biblical community in small group?

4. Where might God be challenging you in the area of stewardship and generosity?

Ongoing assessment. Everyone from an apprentice leader to the executive leadership team at Community Christian Church has someone who is coaching them and meeting with them at least every other week. A part of the ongoing conversation during these one-on-ones are questions about RPMS. These RPMS are as follows:

- Relational
- Physical
- Mental
- Spiritual

In addition, we use six coaching questions to assess how we can be helpful in the development of this person's leadership and their group or team.

In an environment that stresses excellence, how do you teach your leaders to look for integrity before talent?

I'm not sure we do look for integrity before talent. I think we look for people who are moving toward God and willing to be in relationship with us. If those two things are true, we will be able to deal with any issues of integrity. For example, we encourage non-Christians to serve in any area of ministry outside of leadership. Our arts directors even have an in-house slogan, "Let pagans play." We really believe that if we give opportunity for people who are far from God to use their talents while being surrounded by many who are devoted Christ-followers, they will eventually fall in love with Jesus. But for leaders, we hold to our standard of Leadership Expectations.

What safeguards do you have in place to protect and ensure the integrity of your staff?

The best safeguards are consistent and honest conversations in relationships between people who really care about each other. I know that sounds pretty soft and idealistic, but that is what we have at this point. We don't currently have any policies regarding specific issues. We do have a culture where almost all of our one-on-one meetings happen in public places like Starbucks or Panera Bread, or in our conference room with windows. Our offices are arranged in a very open environment, no one has a private office, and everyone kind of knows what's going on with each other. That is a good thing, because any issues that need to be resolved can be resolved quickly when you sit right next to each other.

What advice would you give to the pastor of a smaller church who suspects a key leader may have a character or integrity issue?

First, I would suggest the pastor get counsel or coaching from another pastor or counselor. It is important not to break confidentiality, but I know that when I am going through those kinds of tough issues, it is always helpful to get wise counsel from those who have been through it before. Second, I would encourage them to follow Matthew 18 in pursuit of repentance and reconciliation.

IQ Test

Work through the following questions with the key leaders in your church.

1. How do we screen for integrity in new leaders in our church?

2. How do we ensure new leaders share our core values? How can we improve this process?

3. Has there been an instance in the past when we have promoted talent over integrity? What did we learn? How can we prevent this from happening in the future?

4. What, if any, systems do we have in place for ongoing accountability in our leadership? How can we improve those systems?

5. Are we having the hard conversations with our staff and key leaders? Are any current leaders possibly struggling in the area of personal integrity? How are we going to discuss our concerns with them?

CLINGING TO
A BAD LOCATION

"WE'RE LOCATED UNDER THE FREEWAY
BEHIND THE ABANDONED KMART."

The second oldest adage in real estate is "Location, location, location." (The oldest adage is "Never buy oceanfront property in Arizona," but that's another discussion.) It's interesting to see how many times the issue of finding the right location comes up in the Bible. When Abraham and Lot were parting ways, their biggest decision was "scenic mountaintop lot with spectacular views" or "lush riverfront acreage, dock permit in hand." Lot chose poorly. Peter's first response to seeing Jesus on the mountain with Moses and Elijah was, "What an excellent opportunity to put in multifamily condos." Jesus later explained that he had a more mobile ministry in mind. ("Foxes have holes and birds of the air have nests, but the Son of Man has no place to lay his head.") Of course I'm being facetious, but it's truly amazing how much the right location can impact the growth of an otherwise healthy congregation.

As I shared in *The Multi-Site Church Revolution* (coauthored with Greg Ligon and Warren Bird)[2], we learned this lesson the hard way when Seacoast opened its Greenville, South Carolina, campus. We struggled to find the right location, but all we could find that fit our budget and time frame was the local convention center. The upside was that the meeting space was attractive, there were plenty of rooms for children, and a lot of the equipment we needed for the church was provided by the convention center. There were, however, some challenges. Our first weekend more than three hundred people came; unfortunately, we had parking for ten thousand cars and seating for fifty thousand. To get to our service, you had to walk across the three miles of parking lots and then navigate a maze of 230 separate auditoriums to find us. Not a single housing development was located within a day's drive. We lasted about a month in the convention center before realizing our mistake.

We moved next to a community theater located in the quaint downtown area of Greenville. Like the convention center, the theater had some good points. The parking was convenient, there was a cute secondary theater where we could do children's ministry, and the main auditorium was a beautiful, acoustically perfect venue.

Unfortunately, it was also extremely dark and cavernous; no matter how many people came each weekend, everyone felt like they were the only one there. We had no problem protecting visitors' anonymity; we couldn't see them. We didn't have to worry much about visitors, however. The theater was even farther from the closest neighborhood than the convention center had been.

Finally, we found a nice neighborhood church building that was now a day care center and available on weekends. After upgrading the sound, light, and video systems, redecorating the children's rooms, and remodeling the auditorium, we knew we were home. The campus began to grow and continues to reach new people for Christ on almost a weekly basis. Having the right location doesn't guarantee church growth, but having the wrong location can make it harder than it has to be.

How Do I Know If I Have a Bad Location?

Sometimes it's difficult to determine if your location is negatively impacting the growth of your church. After a while we become accustomed to our building and no longer see the distractions that new attendees might find to be barriers. Let's look at several questions that can help you determine how effective your current location is in helping to fulfill the vision God has given you for your church.

Does Your Location Match Your Mission?

What is the specific God-given mission of your church? Are you called to reach people who look like you? Are you called to a cross-cultural ministry? Do you feel a deep compassion for poor people? Hispanic people? Single people? Young families? NASCAR fans? Obviously we are called to reach everyone with the good news, but your church location may limit your reach. For example, if you lie awake at night troubled by the plight of single mothers living in urban poverty, but your church is located in an affluent suburban neighborhood, your mission may be limited.

When I began feeling the tug to pastor a church, I knew that God was leading me toward a nontraditional ministry. I had never fit in a traditional congregation, and I knew there were thousands of people just like me who would never darken the door of church as they knew it. My vision was to reach out to those people. God was calling me to my personal Judea: middle-class suburbanites who didn't know Jesus.

The challenge I faced is that the church I pastored was not located where people like me lived. It was on a two-lane country road in a small town outside of Houston. Just across the lake was a middle-class Houston suburb called Atascocita, but I soon discovered Lake Houston to be the widest lake in the world. When comparing the two communities, one longtime resident remarked, "They are pretty much the same, except the women in Atascocita are more likely to have all their teeth."

Even though I was pastoring in my own version of Mayberry, I was determined to reach Mount Pilot. I gathered a small team of people who connected to the mission and we shaped a creative, relevant ministry aimed at unchurched suburbanites. We sent out mailers and ran ads in the local paper, and occasionally a few adventurous subdivision dwellers would make the 1.5-mile trek across the dam; but they would quickly retreat to their comfortable neighborhood never to return to our little country church. (I think the greeter with his own spit cup may have scared them off.) The mission was clear, but the location was wrong.

Part of the success we have seen at Seacoast is that our mission clearly matches our neighborhood. We feel strongly that God has called us to reach middle-class suburbanites who don't know Jesus (sound familiar?), and the neighborhoods around our original campus are packed with them. Growing in this location has been relatively easy.

Recently, however, God put a new burden on our hearts. We read in our local newspaper that North Charleston is the seventeenth most dangerous city in America. That is a shocking statistic when you realize how small South Carolina is; we don't have the seventeenth most anything. (If we were a country, Liechtenstein could crush us in a war.) Soon we saw another article that said South Carolina is the most dangerous state in the country. We knew as soon as we read that article that God was calling us to a new mission, so we began looking for the worst location possible to open a new campus. We hit the jackpot when a struggling congregation in a rough neighborhood agreed to share its facility with us. We knew we were in the right place when a police officer stopped by as we were preparing the building for the new campus and told our campus pastor, "You don't know what you're getting into here. There have been two shootings in this neighborhood in the past week. This is the most dangerous street in North Charleston." So now we have a Seacoast campus on the most dangerous street in the most dangerous city in the most dangerous state in America. Every week we feed and clothe hundreds of people while we share the love of Jesus. Our location matches our mission.

Does Your Building Match Your Community?

I live in a typical suburban neighborhood in Charleston. All of the houses look almost exactly the same with vinyl siding, a two-car garage, and an SUV parked in the driveway. At the entrance to my subdivision, however, is a Waffle House. I have nothing against Waffle House; I have eaten Christmas dinner at a Waffle House. (My beautiful wife has not yet forgiven me for that faux pas.) The challenge is that this Waffle House, with its bright yellow sign, 18-wheelers in the parking lot, and 3:00 a.m. breakfast crowd, doesn't exactly fit into our white-picket-fence neighborhood. The neighborhood has formed an uneasy truce with the restaurant since the Waffle House was there first and there's nothing the neighborhood can do about it, but it's not their favorite landmark. I have to admit that I have on occasion snuck in for some hash browns, but hopefully no one saw me. I don't want them to take away my key to the neighborhood swimming pool.

You don't want to be the Waffle House of your neighborhood. It's okay if the gospel is offensive, but your neighbors shouldn't have to wear a disguise to come to your church. Does your church fit into your neighborhood, or is it an eyesore? If you build that new building, will it drop the property values of the houses around you? If everyone in your neighborhood knows *exactly* where you are located because you have been the subject of the last three neighborhood meetings, you may have a bad location.

How Difficult Is It to Find Your Church?

When I lived in Houston, Lakewood Church had the worst location for a church I have ever seen. To get there you had to have a map, a compass, and an armed security guard. You drove through dangerous neighborhoods, made a dozen turns after exiting the freeway, and wound through an industrial park to find the church building. Yet thousands of people attended every weekend. Clearly if you have God's blessing on your church, a great worship experience, and a gifted speaker, location doesn't matter. Of course, it might not hurt to throw in huge billboards on every freeway in the fourth largest city in America and a nationally syndicated television program. (Their billboards at the time read "Lakewood Church: An Oasis of Love." I wanted to put up billboards for our church that read "Church on the Lake: A Puddle of Like." No one else thought it was good idea.) Unless you have hundreds of thousands of dollars to invest in advertising, being in an easily accessible location can have a huge impact on the growth of your church. Can you tell someone from your town how to get to your church without drawing a map? How many turns are you located off the closest major intersection? Do people cringe when you mention your church's neighborhood?

Does Your Building Need Repair?

Imagine driving up to your doctor's office and seeing weeds growing in the parking lot and in the flower beds around the entrance. The paint is peeling on the front door, there is a large water stain on the ceiling of the waiting room, and the smell of mold overwhelms you as you enter. The carpet is threadbare with stains from spilled coffee and other more ominous-looking substances. One of the fluorescent lights is out, and the other one is flickering almost in time with the dragging soundtrack crackling through the ceiling speaker. The couch has several rips, and one of the magazines announces Ronald Reagan's recent election. The water in the aquarium is a moldy green, and on the surface are a couple of floaters who have passed on to goldfish heaven. How do you feel about trusting this doctor with your health? If he puts so little effort into the appearance of his waiting room, how well will he care for you?

That's how new people feel when they drive up to your building and see uncut grass, flower beds in need of weeding, and faded paint. When they go inside and find decor that dates from the 1980s and a sound system that was state-of-the-art when Nixon was still erasing audio tapes, they wonder if anyone is aware that the turn of the century was almost a decade ago. Why would they trust you with their spiritual lives if you don't take care of the things God has already entrusted to you? How could you relate to their lives when you seem to be living in another era?

Your building can be in the right neighborhood, easy to find, and connected to the community, but if it's outdated and in need of repair, it can still be a liability. It doesn't seem very spiritual, but peeling paint, poor lighting, and cheap A/V equipment can be a barrier to sharing the gospel with twenty-first-century Americans.

What Do You Do about a Bad Location?

How committed are you to seeing your church grow? This question is a biggie in considering what to do about a bad location. Changing a location can be one of the hardest, most controversial phases a pastor can lead a church through. The transition is full of risk, and some people will never get on board with it. They don't see the need for a change — the church seems fine the way it is. And they may be right. The church might continue to do what it has always done: grow a little, shrink a little, but always wind up pretty much where it started. If you can be content shepherding the little flock you've been entrusted with, there's no reason to go through the heartburn and turmoil that always accompany major change. But if God has placed a fire in your heart to reach people who may be difficult or impossible to reach without changing your location, you have no choice but to buckle up and take the plunge.

Changing your location begins where every change in your church begins: with your vision. What do you see on the other side of the change? Will God change lives as a result of the transition? Your people will not get behind a change that runs from the past, but they will rally around one that sprints to the future. Whether you are going to paint the Sunday school rooms or move fifteen miles into another neighborhood, you need to have a vision of what the promised land will bring and be able to communicate it in a compelling way to your people. Once you have that vision, it's time to make the change. What change do you need to make?

Fix Up the Present Location

The easiest location change involves simply fixing up the building you are in. It's amazing the difference a little paint, a few flowers, and a couple of new lights can make. The challenge is that very few of us have the kind of budget that it takes to really fix up our buildings. Sometimes, however, we need to look good before we can be good. In other words, we can do cosmetic repairs to our building until we grow enough to raise the money to do the big work. Attack the projects that will improve the look and feel of the building before the projects that will improve the infrastructure. Paint the walls before you replace the roof. Plant flowers before you repave the parking lot.

When Seacoast began sharing a building with a struggling congregation in North Charleston, we sat down with their leaders to discuss some of the improvements we wanted to make. Their list of desired improvements included repaving the parking lot, putting on a new roof, and changing the carpet in the auditorium. While all of these were legitimate needs and should be addressed at some point, we knew that none of these items would help us grow the campus. Instead, we focused on the look and feel of the building. We deployed an army of volunteers who threw away mountains of junk filling several rooms, updated the faded and outmoded paint, and put in new landscaping in the existing flower beds. We took some of the money that we would have spent on a new roof and carpet and instead upgraded the sound system and added theatrical lighting. We were able to get many of the materials and almost all of the labor donated, and we ended up with a very attractive building. The campus now averages almost four hundred people every weekend, and we should be able to address the important but less visible building challenges soon.

Tell People You Are There

Another relatively painless way to improve a bad location is simply to tell people where you are. You may have a great church with a lot to offer, but your community may not know you are there. The most important way to get the word out is for your people to invite their friends, relatives, and neighbors, but there are people in your community they will never touch. You may need to market your church.

A couple of warnings about marketing. First, marketing will not grow your church. Your church will grow when God blesses your ministry and people's lives are changed through that ministry. Marketing may get a bigger crowd to show up once in a while, but the church will grow when people connect to God and to each other. Second, sometimes the only thing worse than your community not knowing about what is happening at your church is for them to find out. If your church service is dreadful (see chapter 3) or your kids' ministry frightens small children (see chapter 4), please don't invite the community. Having a bad experience at your church will simply inoculate visitors against ever returning.

The most basic form of marketing that many churches miss is good, attractive signage. A bright, colorful sign that looks like it was designed in this century will do more to get the word out about your church than any other form of marketing. On the other hand, an outdated marquee displaying pithy sayings (e.g., "Jesus should be your steering wheel, not your spare tire") will do more to keep people away than you could imagine. One of the first things we did at Church on the Lake was to replace the peeling old church sign out on the main road that clearly announced to passersby that we were poor, tacky, and not real smart. I figured people should have to come inside the church to learn some things.

More traditional marketing can be expensive, but if done well it can help let the community know you are there. Outreach Marketing (www.outreach.com) does a great job helping churches create effective marketing tools. One tool we've found effective is business-card-size flyers. For each of our campuses we print attractive business cards with a little information about our church on one side and a map with service times on the back. Our people then use them to invite their friends and neighbors to the church. These cards are inexpensive and our people always have them handy. Another great tool for us is Seacoast T-shirts. When we have events that will involve a lot of our people, we print T-shirts for everyone to wear. Sometimes we sell the shirts, but when we can, we just give them away. These shirts then become living billboards telling our community a little about the church. This strategy is risky in that there is always a possibility that one of our less sanctified attendees will get arrested in a bar fight wearing a Seacoast T-shirt, but it's a risk we are willing to take.

Hit the Road, Jack

Your location may be so horrendous that it's time to hit the road. This is a bold move, but if you want to see the church grow, you may have no other choice. The good news is that you have a lot of options if you decide to call in the moving van.

Go Mobile, Young Man

One of the boldest moves a church can make is to sell its present location and go mobile. There are huge advantages to this strategy. From the sale of the building you will have the capital you need to make some huge upgrades. You will be able to buy good-quality sound, light, and video systems; you might be able to hire an additional staff member; and you will be able to carry out a strong marketing campaign to let the community know where you are. This strategy is risky because the church could wind up with no assets and no people, but the potential is huge. A great resource for churches considering going mobile is *The Nomadic Church* by Bill Easum and Pete Theodore (Abingdon, 2005).

Let's Make a Deal

Another strategy for overcoming a difficult location is to trade buildings with another congregation. When I was young, my dad pastored a church in Denver, Colorado, that met in an unfinished little building in a declining neighborhood. A previous pastor had started the building, but the church had run out of money before completing the work, so the pastor resigned and moved on. After my dad came, the congregation quickly outgrew the building and began to look to build a new facility a few miles away. In the same area where they were looking to build was another congregation with a building they could no longer afford. After a few conversations, it became obvious that the other congregation would fit very well in our little building and their larger building would give us room to grow. The trade became a blessing for both congregations.

Do We Stay or Do We Go?

When The Oaks Fellowship in Dallas, Texas, built a new facility several miles from its original location, the leaders made a bold decision: they decided to go and to stay. Rather than selling their original location and moving everything farther into the suburbs, they decided to keep a presence there and change the services to better match the more urban community. They became one church in two locations with two very distinct visions of ministry. They were able to leverage the synergy of shared resources while also reaching two distinct cultural groups at the same time. As The Oaks Fellowship has grown, the church has had more and more opportunities to plant congregations into existing church facilities and become one church in many locations. God may be calling your church to stay *and* to go.

Architectural Evangelism

An obvious relocation choice is to sell your building and build one in a more desirable location, but before you start the capital campaign, consider another option. There may be an empty building in your community that would make a great new location for your congregation. Do we really need another church building in America? Are we being good stewards of the resources God has given us by cutting down more trees and turning acres of nature into parking lots? Sometimes I think pastors are more interested in building a permanent shrine to their legacy than positively representing the kingdom of God.

At Seacoast we have adopted a philosophy of architectural evangelism. Before we even consider building a new building, we look for an existing building that we can redeem. We are currently using two church buildings that other congregations have moved out of, a former Food Lion supermarket, a warehouse, a former technology company call center, and two movie theaters. The only building we have built is at our original campus, and there were no empty buildings when we started in the community twenty years ago.

All over the country churches are moving into existing buildings and redeeming the architecture. My in-laws' church in St. Louis just moved into a car dealership. (I think they are offering trade-ins on used sins and excellent financing on an 8 percent tithe.) Fellowship Church in Dallas has a campus in a furniture store and another in a dilapidated warehouse dating back to the 1930s. Pathways Church in Denver bought a former Jewish temple in an urban neighborhood and is leading a movement of community transformation from its new home base. A great building for your church may already exist; you just need to make some modifications and move in.

Location Paralysis

One of the regrets I have from my days of pastoring Church on the Lake is that I took the easy way out. When we arrived at the church, it was in terrible shape. Some of the doors were rotting, the outside paint was peeling, and the carpet was worn and musty. The church was located on a meandering road in a community that was shrinking. I knew that the only way the church would flourish was if we either moved it or improved the current building. We chose the easier course and fixed up the building we already had. We repainted and relit and recarpeted everything, and in the end we had a very cute little church in the woods. But I'll always wonder what would have happened had I made the bold move to reach the community I felt God had called us to. Don't let location paralysis keep you from fulfilling the vision God has given you for your church.

My brother Greg, founding pastor of Seacoast Church, is one of the most insightful church planters in the United States. Pastors from across the country call him for input on major decisions their congregations are trying to make, so I thought he'd have great insight into how your church can improve its location.

•••••••••••••••••••••**SPOTLIGHT**•••••••••••••••••••••

Greg Surratt, Seacoast Church

I am often asked what it is like working for my brother Greg Surratt. On the one hand, he is a good boss, a talented leader, and a visionary. On the other hand, he used to put me in painful wrestling holds until Mom would make him let me go. Since Mom made him start being nice to me a couple of years ago, working together at Seacoast has been a great experience. We try to keep the ministry and family stuff separate, but we are also able to cut through some of the communication barriers quicker than others because we are brothers. (Let's just say we occasionally have intense fellowship.) Nepotism seems to work, at least for us.

Greg started Seacoast in 1988 with a group of about sixty people out of Northwood Assembly in Charleston, South Carolina. Each year for the first three years, the church averaged fewer people on the weekends than the year before, but in 1991 the church began to grow and never stopped. Today more than nine thousand people attend each weekend in thirteen locations across three states. During the growth Greg has become a student of what will and will not lead a church to grow, and he has had the opportunity to share that knowledge with hundreds of church planters and pastors. I knew he would have insight into finding the right location for your church.

What is the worst church location you have seen?

A church planter came to ask my advice one time about a location he was looking at in his community. He said that it was easy to find, had good visibility, ample parking, a great auditorium, some side rooms for kids, the price was right, and to top it all off it was nearly new and immediately available.

I asked him where one might find such a choice piece of real estate, to which he replied that it was actually a funeral home. "Not good," I thought. "No wonder it's available."

How do you explain to a well-meaning, naive, amped-up church planter that a place so closely associated with death is probably not the best choice of locations to plant a "life-giving" church? I have friends who won't even go to their friends' funerals because the thought of being where dead people are creeps them out. How are you going to get them to come to a place like that weekly? Sounds like a marketer's nightmare. Let's use common sense here. He didn't listen, and within a few months they wrote the obituary for the once promising vision.

How important is a good location to the growth of a church?

In retail it is location, location, location. In church work I would argue that it is Spirit of God, Spirit of God, Spirit of God. But, that said, location is pretty high on the rest of the list.

I think that God primarily draws people to himself and to our churches, but part of our job as leaders is to remove potential barriers that stand in the way of people finding their way to God. Location is definitely a biggie when it comes to barriers. If you can't find it, or wouldn't want to go there if you could find it, that poses a pretty big barrier. So I'd say location is pretty important.

How important was Seacoast's location to the growth in the early days?

When we were looking for a permanent location for Sea-coast, we wanted something that would allow us to be both local and regional. Pretty presumptuous for a group of two hundred people, but they don't charge extra for big dreams. Local meant that there were neighborhoods close by; we could actually be a part of the community. If it was too local, though, buried too deep in a neighborhood and not close to major traffic routes, we would have a hard time reaching beyond it. Regional meant that it was accessible to more than just the local neighborhoods. People could easily drive from other communities, so we weren't limited to just the few blocks around us. If it was too regional, it would be easy to get to, but no one would live there. Think airports, factory areas, and coliseums. Unless you are Joel Osteen, and you are not, it still might not be the ideal location until your attendance is about ten thousand or so. We've made mistakes being too regional with new campus plants. Easy to get to, but nobody lived there.

I think our choice of location definitely made an impact on both early growth and future growth. We researched where we thought traffic patterns and housing starts would trend toward. It is still a great location that is easily accessible to most of the Charleston area.

What makes a bad location?

Lots of factors make a bad location: you can't find it, you wouldn't want to go there if you could find it, no one lives there (and probably won't anytime soon), the neighborhood doesn't match the vision of the church trying to minister to it.

What advice would you give to pastors whose churches are "stuck" in a bad location? What practical steps can they take?

Move on. Sometimes the best thing you can do is throw in the towel and go somewhere else. About ten years into the Seacoast experience, I had the bright idea of doing church in a larger auditorium that happened to be a Masonic Temple. At the risk of sounding disparaging to both Masons and temples, it turned out to be a very scary place. Being a visionary, I saw only the potential — more room, better parking, easy accessibility — and ignored the huge downsides — children's ministry would be done in a bar, frightening pictures in the foyer, occasional raffles and events that would supersede church services. I even brought in Peter Wagner to pray over the temple, and then I declared it a perfect fit for Seacoast. After six months of pushing a rope uphill, I finally admitted that the "temple of doom" experiment was less than successful. I ate some Southern-fried crow and we moved on. If you are in a bad location and you can do it, move on, but if you can't . . .

Get God's heart. If you are truly stuck, then it is possible that

God has a plan for you and your place of ministry that you are not aware of yet. It will probably involve a change in the way you are doing things. We seldom change just because it is a good idea, so part of the "stuckness" may be a nudge toward being open to something different. I know a pastor who felt stuck. He didn't feel fulfilled in what he was doing nor very fruitful in ministry; very few people were coming, and he felt like he couldn't move somewhere else. So, as a last resort, he sought God — what a novel idea — and got a fresh vision for his community. The vision involved changing the way they did ministry and reaching out to a segment of the community they had previously ignored. Now they've had to move a few blocks away to a public school because the numbers of people they are reaching won't fit into their previous location. Always remember your ministry location is never a surprise to God. He may very well have you where you are because he desperately cares about the people who live there and he wants to recommission you to reach them. But it probably won't be with the same old, same old. Sometimes the best thing you can do with a bad location is to get a fresh vision.

IQ Test

Discuss the following questions with some key leaders in your church. Consider bringing in real estate agents, builders, and retail business owners to help inform the discussion.

1. Does your church's location match the mission of your church?

2. Does your building match your community?

3. How difficult is it to find your church? Do people in your community know you are there? What could you do to raise community awareness of your church?

4. Does your building need repair? What are the top three items that should be addressed immediately? What are the top three long-term items that need to be addressed as soon as possible?

5. Should you consider changing locations? If you were to move, what would be an ideal location? Brainstorm creative possibilities for moving to a new location.

7

COPYING ANOTHER SUCCESSFUL CHURCH

"AFTER THE LAST CHURCH GROWTH CONFERENCE WE CHANGED
OUR NAME TO WILLOWBACK FELLOWSHIP CHURCH."

One of the pivotal events in my ministry was the first Willow Creek conference I attended. I had never been to a megachurch before; just driving onto the campus was a life-changing experience. I'll never forget winding down the beautifully landscaped road until we reached acres of parking lots. (I expected to see a monorail and cartoon signs designating the Strobel, Beach, and Hybels lots.) We entered the massive lobby where dozens of attractive, smiling volunteers offered to help us with any need that might arise. Working my way through the crowded lobby into the auditorium, I found a seat among the thousands of other conference attendees. While I waited for the session to begin, I stared at the rows and rows of theatrical lights, huge video screens, and massive windows overlooking a private pond full of ducks. Was this heaven? No, I was reassured, this was Illinois.

The first session opened with a poignant, funny drama. The lights faded down stage right and up stage left on a talented soloist singing "Show Me the Way" by the band Styx. I had never been to Broadway, but I couldn't imagine anything more professional. Other than an occasional choir cantata, I had never seen drama used in church, and I'd certainly never heard a secular song used to set up a sermon. That morning as Bill Hybels preached that lost people matter to God and that our job is to create a safe place where they can hear the gospel, I was hooked. I felt at home at Willow Creek like no other church I had ever attended. I knew this was *exactly* what I was supposed to do with the rest of my life. My challenge was that I didn't think the church where I was youth pastor was ready for Styx on Sunday morning. On the way home from the conference, I began to dream of how I would "do church" when my opportunity came.

I got my chance a couple of years later when I became a pastor in Huffman, Texas (population eight thousand). By this time I had been to another Willow Creek conference and had visited the church's weekend services. I read everything Bill Hybels wrote and listened to every one of his sermon tapes. I was ready to bring Willow Creek to rural Texas. The first weekend after I became the pastor, we held an all-church workday. I had the parishioners pull all of the hymnals out of the pews and stack them on the sidewalk outside the sanctuary. Toward the end of the day, sweet little old Sister Dolly asked me, "Pastor Surratt, what are we going to do with the hymn books?" With all of the seeker-sensitive passion I could muster, I informed her we were taking the hymnals to the landfill. She looked as though I had slapped her favorite kitten, but she dutifully grabbed an armload of sacred music and headed for the dumpster. And so began the Willow Creek Goes Rural experiment.

Doing drama turned out to be problematic. I quickly discovered that classically trained actors are easier to come by in Chicago than in Huffman. We had wonderful volunteers willing to do whatever it took to reach people for Jesus, but frankly, they just looked frightened onstage. Using secular tunes was a challenge as well. I thought "Life in the Fast Lane" was a great idea for a song to kick off a series on surviving the rat race; but when you are unemployed, are living on welfare, and listen only to country music, the Eagles aren't as relevant as you would think they might be. For the first few months of Willow Creek meets Hick Lake, my little congregation was mostly stunned. They liked me, but for the love of all that was good, they couldn't figure out what I was doing.

The sermons were the worst part. I was channeling Bill Hybels. I would either listen to one of his sermons or read a chapter in one of his books and then try to reproduce it in the pulpit that weekend. I knew I was in trouble when I shared how I had led the first mate on my racing yacht to Jesus during a regatta on Lake Michigan. (I didn't even know what a regatta is.)

I was rescued when I heard Rick Warren speak for the first time. Now here was a guy I could copy. He even said that if his bullet fit my gun, I could shoot it. I didn't own a gun, but I got the idea. I immediately bought all of Rick's books and subscribed to his sermon tapes. Overnight we went from seeker-sensitive to purpose-driven. We quit doing dramas and secular songs, and all of my sermons became five steps to success or four keys to freedom. I didn't start wearing Hawaiian shirts, but I did take off my tie. To my congregation's relief, they didn't have to sit through any more incomprehensible dramas and the sermons were a lot easier to follow (Rick is a *lot* easier to copy than Bill), but they were still confused. I hadn't discovered God's unique vision for our unique community using my unique gifts and talents. I'm not sure we ever did in my two and half years as their pastor.

One of the great things about being a pastor in America today is the plethora (I love that word) of resources available. There are hundreds of books explaining how you can grow your church (none as good as this book, obviously), and there is a church conference to attend almost every week. The temptation is to simply adopt someone else's vision or methodology and impose it on our own churches. And then we choose up teams according to which megachurch we are currently emulating. The conversation goes something like this:

"What's Bob doing these days?"

"He went to the Drive Conference last year and now he's doing the North Point thing."

"Wow, that's expensive. Moving lights, fog, high-definition video?"

"Yep, the whole package. What do you hear about Steve? I haven't seen him since seminary."

"He's emerging."

"Hmm. I never saw Steve as a candles and chanting kind of guy. What about ..."

"Cursing during his sermon? Oh yeah. He's all in. What about you?"

"I think we're just going to stick with seeker-sensitive with a side of outwardly focused, at least until the dust settles on this whole emerging thing."

Learning without Leaning

I thank God for the leadership and courage of pastors like Bill Hybels, Rick Warren, Andy Stanley, and many others. They have helped

countless churches around the world through their teaching, conferences, and writing. I continue to learn from them as well as from the
other pastors featured throughout this book. If we weren't learning
from other pastors, we would miss out on the excellent resources that
God has blessed the church with in the twenty-first century. We now
have access to books, conferences, and podcasts on a daily basis that
can instruct, correct, and inspire us to lead our churches in new and
unique ways. I believe we can reach more people with the gospel and
be more effective at making disciples by building on the knowledge
of pastors who are further down the road than we are.

The challenge is when we stop learning and start leaning; when
we try to simply copy what we've seen in another successful ministry.
Each one of us has been created in a unique way and given unique
resources to reach a unique community. One of the theme verses of
my life comes from Paul's letter to the Ephesian church: "For we are
God's workmanship, created in Christ Jesus to do good works, which
God prepared in advance for us to do" (Eph. 2:10).

God has created each one of us as an individual work of art with
a unique purpose in this world. He needs us to lead the specific ministry in the way he has wired us to lead. Paul knew God had sent
him to the Gentiles because of his unique gifting and background.
He couldn't simply imitate what he had learned from Peter, James,
and Barnabas; he had to become the leader God had created him to
be. Let's look at three basic questions to help us unpack how we can
follow Paul's example and find the unique niche God has created us
to fill.

Who Are You?

Every pastor has to answer this fundamental question. I began
by admitting that I am not Bill Hybels, I am not Rick Warren, and
I am not Andy Stanley. While I learned from their ministries, I had
to stop trying to preach their sermons and copying their ministry
style. One of the biggest turning points in the life of the church was

when Paul realized he was called to preach to the Gentiles and Peter realized he was created to preach to the Jews. How has God uniquely wired you?

One place to start is to understand your personality. Are you a people person, an analytical type, a party animal, an introvert, or a Cubs fan? (I'm not sure God can use you if you are a Cubs fan; something must be intrinsically wrong with someone who can believe year after year in such a futile cause.) What pumps you up? What saps your energy? What kind of people do you love to work with? What kind of people make you cringe when they walk into the room?

Many great resources are available to help you find out more about you. One of the first I read was *Please Understand Me* by David Keirsey and Marilyn Bates; this book gives insight through the Myers-Briggs personality assessment. Another great resource is the DISC Profile, which is available from a variety of sources. (Just google "DISC Profile" and you will get fifty thousand results. One of those websites should work.) The insights from these tools have helped me better understand what God created me to be.

Another great tool for learning how you can strategically leverage the gifts God has given you is *Now Discover Your Strengths* by Marcus Buckingham and Donald O. Clifton. The premise of the book as applied to pastors is that we should spend most of our time building on our strengths rather than trying to eliminate our weaknesses. For me this means that I should work to sharpen the gifts God has given me to preach, teach, and write and not worry too much about the fact that I can't find my keys. It works out well that I live a little more than a mile from my office; I can always walk to work.

The final but most important tool I have found helpful is a spiritual gifts inventory. While each of the gift inventories I have taken over the years seems to have a different theological bent, I have found them very useful in helping me shape the ministry that I do and the ministry that I don't do. I discovered several years ago that I do not have a strong mercy gift. Actually, I have no mercy gift at all, so I do very few hospital visits. My hospital conversations often go something like this:

"Hey, Jim, how are you doing? You look terrible."

"I feel terrible. The doctors can't figure out what's wrong."

"Bummer …"

Long, uncomfortable pause.

"We should probably pray or something."

Almost no one gets better when I visit them in the hospital.

My mercy gift deficiency combined with a lack in the "word of wisdom" area makes counseling problematic as well. My natural response when people tell me their problems is, "Wow, what are you going to do about that?" You'd be surprised how few people find solace or direction in that kind of advice.

I spent my early years of ministry beating myself up over these shortcomings and vowing to get better, but I eventually realized it just wasn't in me. God had not created me to be a traditional pastor and counselor. I certainly have to improve these skills, and I have actually learned to love people (well, like them a lot), but now I try to spend my time working in the areas of my gifts and strengths and finding ways to empower others who have the gifts of mercy and words of wisdom to operate in their strengths. We have leaders in our church who love to visit people in the hospital. They know just the right thing to say, they know how to pray the prayer of faith, and at the end of a day of hospital visits, they feel energized. A full day of hospital visits might drive me to find solace with my new friend Jack Daniels. If I did too many hospital visits, I would not only raise the mortality rate in our congregation; I would be standing in the way of others fulfilling their God-given purpose on earth.

So don't build your ministry around what's hot or who is successful, and don't try to be the stereotype of what you think a pastor should look like. While we all have to operate out of our "green zone" at times (I'm sure John the Baptist preferred desert crusades to prison ministry), God has given each of us unique strengths and gifts. Focus on those and gather people around you who can make up for your weaknesses.

What Can't You Stand?

The plot of every Popeye cartoon was always the same: Popeye's archenemy Bluto would irritate Popeye until he finally uttered his famous line, "I've had all I can stand. I can't stands no more." Popeye would then eat a whole can of spinach in a single bite and whip up on poor Bluto. Bill Hybels, in his book *Holy Discontent*, calls such an occurrence a "Popeye Moment."[3]

What is your Popeye Moment? What can't you stands no more? What do you see in the world around you that drives you crazy? What occupies your thoughts every day? What do you most want to see change for the people in your community? Paul says in Philippians 2:13 (NLT), "For God is working in you, giving you the desire and the power to do what pleases him." God has placed deep inside each of us a discontent with what we see in the world. What is your discontent?

For you it may be the fact that people are lost and facing an eternity without Jesus. Every evangelical pastor feels this discontent to some extent, but for some it is a consuming passion. If that describes you, then you need to focus your energy on evangelism. Maybe you can't stand the fact that so many people who commit their lives to Christ never grow up in their faith. Your church should center its ministry on discipleship. Or you may be wired like my friend Dino Rizzo, who pastors Healing Place Church in Baton Rouge, Louisiana. Dino can't stand the fact that there are families around his church who don't have access to decent health care, single moms who can't afford to buy clothes for their children, and teenagers who don't have a safe place to sleep at night. So the mission statement of Dino's church is to be a "Healing Place for a hurting world." It is much more than a statement on a masthead; it is a way of life. Every day Healing Place Church provides food, shelter, and medical care for hundreds of people in the community. Dino has turned his God-given discontent into community-transforming ministry. Has God wired you like Dino with a passion to transform your community?

Clearly every church should be involved in evangelism, discipleship, and community outreach; the question is where you will spend the majority of your time. Some would say that your church should be balanced in each of these areas. Sometimes we equate balance with health, but people and churches that accomplish big things are seldom equally balanced in all areas. They find their passion, their divine dissatisfaction, and lean into it. Peter seemed anything but balanced as he tossed aside his fishing nets and passionately pursued Christ. The Acts church doesn't sound particularly balanced in this passage: "All the believers were together and had everything in common. Selling their possessions and goods, they gave to anyone as he had need. Every day they continued to meet together in the temple courts. They broke bread in their homes and ate together with glad and sincere hearts, praising God and enjoying the favor of all the people. And the Lord added to their number daily those who were being saved" (Acts 2:44 – 47).

That sounds like a pretty radical group of people living out the passion that God had placed deep inside each of them. If you want to see your church grow, find the passion that God planted in you years ago and use every resource you can get your hands on to change your corner of the world.

Where Is Your Church?

The point of this question is not the physical address of your church building (if you cannot find your church, you may want to reread chapter 6 on clinging to a bad location), but the makeup of the community where God has placed your congregation. I missed this when I tried to pattern my little rural Texas church after a cutting-edge ministry located in the suburbs of Chicago and an affluent congregation in the fastest-growing county in California. Willow Creek and Saddleback did an excellent job of understanding their communities and building relevant ministries to reach out to the seekers all around them. The problem I ran into was that Unchurched Harry and Saddleback Sam didn't live in Huffman, Texas; we were surrounded by Redneck Bubba and Unemployed Eddie. Rather than adopting a model of ministry designed to reach a community hundreds of miles away, I should have been studying the distinctive community where God had planted me.

To be effective in our place of ministry, we must first come to an intimate knowledge of the surrounding community. Ed Stetzer and David Putman describe it this way in their excellent book *Breaking the Missional Code: Your Church Can Become a Missionary in Your Community*: "[Missionaries] know that they must have a profound understanding of their host culture before planning a strategy to reach the unique cultural group that exists in that cultural context. This is why they first study the culture to find strategies that will work among the people who live in that cultural setting."[4]

What is the unique cultural setting of your church? Are you in an urban setting in a changing neighborhood? Are you in a rapid-growth suburb within a huge metropolitan area? Are the socioeconomic factors in your community static or changing? What is the racial makeup of your community? No outside model of ministry will fit perfectly into your context; the hard work of ministry is to understand how God is calling you to influence your community.

Identifying our cultural context has proven to be a challenge for us at Seacoast Church. We have campuses in thirteen distinctly different communities spread across three states. While we currently use the same weekend message at each campus, the individual expressions of ministry are very different from congregation to congregation. I told the story earlier of our campuses located in the most dangerous city in South Carolina. We have seen prostitutes soliciting business on the sidewalk, drug dealers making sales in the parking lot, and teenagers gunned down within a couple of blocks of the church. Our ministry looks very different there than it does at our original site located in an affluent suburb of Charleston. One of the differences is our Adopt-a-Block program (which we patterned after the Dream Center in Los Angeles — www.dreamcenter.org), in which a team of volunteers goes door-to-door every other Saturday asking if there are any needs we can help with or anything we can pray with the residents about. Our teams help clean up trash, paint houses, and repair broken cars. Each week more and more community members are venturing into the church for the very first time. If we went door-to-door in the neighborhoods around our original suburban campus, the residents would call the police on us.

A surface understanding of your community combined with a hit-and-run mentality of evangelism can actually do more harm than good. A few years ago some of our members heard a sermon about servant evangelism through random acts of kindness. They got very excited as they thought about where they could deploy their new weapon of mass evangelism. They settled on a predominantly African-American community located not far from their mostly white, entirely suburban campus. These well-meaning Christians surmised that this community would be overwhelmed by free handouts from their more affluent neighbors. The only question was what freebie should they offer? Finally, a lightbulb came on — literally; they would give away lightbulbs. They began collecting packages of lightbulbs and planning their assault. The appointed Saturday arrived and several dozen caring white people loaded up their SUVs and Volvo station wagons and headed off for their first intentional act of random kindness. They spread out across the neighborhood and began ringing doorbells, offering free lightbulbs to whoever came to the door. They were shocked by the reactions, which ranged from confusion to shock to outright anger. It seems that the proud neighborhood, established by freed slaves at the end of the Civil War, wasn't looking for charity from neighbors who didn't even know their names. And they had all the lightbulbs they needed, thank you very much.

The would-be servant evangelists retreated to their comfortable vinyl-clad houses and rethought their strategy. They realized that they had made assumptions without forming relationships and had probably done more damage than good. But they didn't give up. They continued to reach out to the community and to form relationships with the community leaders. They learned that while the neighborhood had plenty of lightbulbs, what it really needed were repairs to the athletic fields and community center. The lightbulb brigade immediately became a construction crew. They partnered with craftsmen within the community and, working side by side, transformed the basketball court, softball diamond, and community center into nice facilities for neighborhood children. In the process they laid the foundation for an ongoing relationship of mutual trust and respect. I think Jesus called it being salt and light.

Who's Not Going to Church?

Your community has some great churches; churches that rightly divide the Word of truth, churches that worship God in spirit and in truth, churches that proclaim the love of Jesus to a lost and dying world. So what is the point of your church? Why does your church need to exist if there are already other churches in your community doing a good (possibly better) job of everything your church is trying to do? These are depressing questions, so very few pastors think through the implications. Wouldn't it make sense for many American churches to just close their doors and send their members to another church in town?

My answer is possibly yes. If we are going to keep our focus on gathering more and more sheep into our sheep pen by collecting as many sheep as possible from other meadows around town, there is no reason to maintain so many buildings, pay so many pastors, and support so many bloated ministries. If, however, we stop worrying about whose meadow the sheep are eating in this weekend and start worrying about all of the sheep who have no shepherd, then we will never have too many churches.

The reality is that your community needs your church. There are people in your neighborhood who will never respond to the tug of Jesus on their hearts if your congregation did not exist. The key is to stop worrying about who is going to church and start focusing on who does not attend church. How can your church uniquely reach out to people no one else is reaching? Rather than copying other churches, use what you learn to become the unique instrument that God created you to be in your community.

Scott Chapman and Jeff Griffin, copastors of The Chapel in suburban Chicago, have the unique challenge of building a distinct ministry in the shadow of one of the best-known churches in America. I asked Scott to help us understand how they have navigated the waters of learning without copying.

• • • • • • • • • • • • • • • • • • • **SPOTLIGHT** • • • • • • • • • • • • • • • •

Scott Chapman, The Chapel

When I heard that The Chapel, a nondenominational church located in suburban Chicago, was planning to launch four new campuses on the same day, I knew I had to meet these guys. Anyone that audacious is either very sharp or very crazy; either way, meeting them would be fun. A mutual friend, Jim Tomberlin, who pioneered the regional strategy at Willow Creek, set up a trip for some of the leaders at The Chapel to visit us in Charleston. We met at Sticky Fingers Rib House (they have the best ribs south of Memphis — don't miss it when you come to see me), and I learned just how audacious *and* crazy these guys are.

The Chapel was started in 1994 by Jeff and Scott, who share the role of senior pastor. (I was going to write about sharing the role of pastor as the eleventh stupid thing until I met Jeff and Scott.) Since our first meeting over ribs and sweet tea, The Chapel has transitioned from gathering in a single location to meeting across five different campuses. One campus emerged when a local church decided to join The Chapel and grew from eight hundred to more than sixteen hundred. A second campus came about when a small mainline church asked to become a part of what The Chapel was doing. That struggling church of fifty has grown to a thriving campus of almost five hundred. A third campus was born out of an empty church building and now has four hundred weekly attendees. A fourth campus was launched in the county jail, where more than 150 inmates and their families are ministered to by two dedicated full-time staff. Including the original campus, about five thousand people currently attend The Chapel every weekend.

Over the past several years, I have had the opportunity to interact with Scott, Jeff, and the other leaders at The Chapel through a "leadership community" that I facilitated for Leadership Network. I've been impressed by their ability to learn from other churches while maintaining their individual identity. I asked Scott recently to explain how they maintain this balance.

How has the ministry of your church been impacted by learning from other churches?

The Chapel has been dramatically influenced by the broader Christian stream from its very beginnings. We have always sought out innovators and effective practitioners; churches like Willow Creek, Saddleback, and North Point in Atlanta have been very formative for us along the way. Most recently, our church leaped from one to five campuses over the span of a few short months. We would have never been able to contemplate such a move without the wisdom and guidance of churches that have led the way in this movement. In particular, Seacoast, LifeChurch.tv, North Coast, and Community Christian Church all helped us to understand the complexity of a multicampus operation. Truthfully, we are the beneficiaries of all their hard-won experience.

Do you feel you have ever tried too hard to copy another successful ministry?

Before Jeff and I started The Chapel, both he and I had

the opportunity to serve as associate pastors in several other churches. In some of those churches, a very heavy emphasis was placed on copying a successful church's model and style of ministry. The idea was to follow in the wake of an effective innovator and assume that their unique ministry success would translate directly into our environment. The results were nothing less than disastrous. We had not gone through the same process of being led by God into those same innovative conclusions. Rather, we had tried to borrow from someone else's experience with God. God must first transform the leader before he can transform the church. There is a journey that each pastor must travel before their church can follow God down that same path.

Not only that, but we failed to understand that each church exists in a unique time and place, and it is essential that we give God the freedom to do what he wants, where he wants, and in the way that he wants to do it. There are many different God-honoring approaches to ministry, but for each church there is only one God-led way. Churches achieve their full redemptive potential not just when they honor God, but when they allow him to lead them into the heart of their community.

How do you find the unique ministry God has called you to in the midst of studying other churches?

We have discovered that God is calling every church to walk down a unique path with him. From a kingdom perspective, it is important to consider the people God has placed within one's own sphere of influence. Every community has a certain identity, a specific cultural expression, and a distinct set of needs. God meets people where they are by shaping each church's ministry to meet the needs of their community in a way that demonstrates his reality, his relevance, and his love. Having said that, there are many principles that we can learn from how ministry is done in other settings. Allowing the effectiveness of other ministries to sharpen our own allows us to benefit from what God has taught others. Inevitably, however, there comes a moment in the life of every leader in every church when they have to take on a posture of openness and dependence on God and seek his unique will for their church and community. There is no substitute for a leader's time alone with God, seeking his direction and his heart for the community in which they live.

How do you learn from other churches? How do you filter this information to find application for your church?

From the very beginning, The Chapel has been a church that has invested a substantial amount of effort in seeking out the leading edge of Christianity. In addition to attending conferences, immersing ourselves in the latest publications, and processing current issues, every year we try to visit a single metropolitan area in which Christ is doing some unique and impacting things. In those cities, we set up a series of meetings and attempt to learn from the leaders of those churches to better understand how God is bringing change. At several points in our history, there has been a significant change in course that God has been calling us to make. At each of those points, not only did we seek out the leaders in those arenas, but we spent time carefully considering and praying through different perspectives on the same issue. We have always believed that the tension created from different approaches to the same issue creates an environment where we are more likely to find the unique calling that God has for us.

When we first began to consider a multicampus strategy, we took the time to meet with all the leaders of the multisite movement. From them, we learned a spectrum of very different approaches that were attempting to address the same issue. That process of understanding the similarities and differences between how godly, effective leaders were pursuing the same vision forced us to ask questions about our own identity, our unique environment, and the specific calling that God had placed on our church.

If you were pastoring a smaller congregation with limited resources, what would you do to learn from other churches? How would you apply what you learned without becoming a church clone?

Our early years reflected the experience of many small churches around the country. We started without any people, any funds, or any facility. In those days, every penny counted and every person wore many hats. The grand visions presented at large conferences seemed inapplicable to where we were. Often we had a few people attend a conference and purchase the recordings from the sessions that spoke most directly to our situation. From there, we would create an experience back at our church for our staff, elders, and key leaders. We would use those resources to develop the thinking of our people and start them on a process of spiritual discovery. We wanted them to understand what those things meant for us now, but even more importantly, what they would mean for us later. We understood that God could do remarkable things through any size church. Our size was not nearly as important as our ability to invest in people and open them up to anything that God may want them to do.

Don't let the size of your congregation or the resources available determine the vision God has given you. Learn from other successful churches, leverage that knowledge within your unique context, and invest in the people God has placed in your care. Don't ever forget that God is able to do more than you could possibly ask or imagine.

IQ Test

Take some time alone to think through the following questions. Once you have a clear feel for what God is saying to you in this area, discuss your answers with your inner circle of leaders.

1. Describe your personality. Are you a people person or an introvert? Someone who likes to analyze or someone with a bent for action? What pumps you up? What saps your energy? What kind of people do you love to work with? What kind of people make you cringe when they walk into the room?

2. What are you passionate about? What can't you stand about this world? What do you wake up at night wanting to change?

3. What is the unique cultural context of your church? Are you in an urban setting in a changing neighborhood? Are you in a rapid-growth suburb within a huge metropolitan area? Are the socioeconomic factors in your community static or changing? What is the racial makeup of your community?

4. What segment of your community is your church uniquely gifted and called to reach? How are you reaching that segment? What do you need to change to reach these people?

5. What do you know about the people who do not attend church in your community? Have they ever attended church? Why don't they attend now? How can you learn more about them?

8

FAVORING DISCIPLINE
OVER RECONCILIATION

"I FELT GUILTY ASKING MOM TO LEAVE THE CHURCH,
BUT SOMETIMES YOU HAVE TO MAKE THE TOUGH CALL."

A friend of mine pastors a church of fifty people. He has pastored several churches in the time I have known him and every church eventually averages fifty people. I'm pretty sure he will always pastor a church of fifty people. The interesting thing is that he seldom pastors the same fifty people from year to year, so there is certainly variety. The pattern is almost always the same. My friend, we'll call him Pastor Bob, will move to a new church in a new community. He will spend a lot of time getting to know the people in the church; he will visit them in the hospital, officiate at their parents' funerals, and perform their children's weddings. Pastor Bob will invite people in town to his church, and the congregation will begin to grow. Everyone loves Pastor Bob and everyone comments that they have never had a pastor like him. Before long Pastor Bob's church has grown to sixty, seventy, even eighty people.

And then it happens: someone in the congregation has to be confronted. Someone is stirring up trouble in the church. An attendee may be spreading rumors about Pastor Bob, a leader may be living in sin, or a deacon just won't get with the program. Whatever the cause, Pastor Bob knows what has to be done. He sets up a meeting with the offending member and confronts this individual with his or her misdeed. This meeting seldom goes well; few people like to be confronted with their shortcomings. Sometimes the censured members decide to leave the church; sometimes Pastor Bob asks them to leave the church. When they leave, they take several families with them. Soon the church is down to seventy members, then sixty, and finally fifty. Pastor Bob would love to see his church grow beyond fifty, but he can't just ignore issues that require church discipline, can he?

The apostle Paul was very clear that church discipline is serious business. When he heard about sin in the congregation at Corinth, this was his response: "Even though I am not physically present, I am with you in spirit. And I have already passed judgment on the one who did this, just as if I were present. When you are assembled in the name of our Lord Jesus and I am with you in spirit, and the power of our Lord Jesus is present, hand this man over to Satan, so that the sinful nature may be destroyed and his spirit saved on the day of the Lord" (1 Cor. 5:3 – 5).

Paul wanted the Corinthians to understand that sin in the congregation is serious business and has to be dealt with seriously. As I mentioned in chapter 5, however, he was dealing with a man who was sleeping with his stepmother (speaking for all of us who have stepmothers, ick!), and everyone in the church knew what was going on. I don't think Paul believed that most offenses merited such a harsh reaction. Even in a case this outrageous and disgusting, Paul indicates in his next letter that grace should be the final word: "The punishment inflicted on him by the majority is sufficient for him. Now instead, you ought to forgive and comfort him, so that he will not be overwhelmed by excessive sorrow. I urge you, therefore, to reaffirm your love for him" (2 Cor. 2:6 – 8).

Paul indicates that the overriding factor in dealing with difficult or wayward church members is love expressed through grace and mercy and that with repentance comes restoration. He says that while sin must be confronted, the goal of that confrontation should always be full reconciliation and restoration to the body. If Paul recommended restoration for a perverted church member who slept with his father's wife, I bet he would let Brother Billy back into your church even if he did call you a stubborn mule at your last board meeting.

Biting Sheep Syndrome

While there are certainly times we have to deal with obvious, unrepented sin in the flock (we'll talk more about this later in the chapter), often we are simply dealing with biting sheep. We lead, we pray, we care for the little lambs, and they respond by criticizing our leadership, second-guessing our decisions, and informing everyone we aren't feeding them like their last shepherd did. The natural reaction when bitten is to bite back, beat the sheep about the head and shoulders with your shepherd's staff, or invite the sheep to find a fold they like better. Often when pastors get together, they share scars from sheep bites and fantasize about an all-church mutton roast. So how do you respond to biting sheep with grace and mercy? How can you keep even sheep with a taste for pastor meat in the fold? We can follow Jesus' example.

Have you ever thought about all the problems Jesus' disciples gave him? James and John were constantly jockeying for a better seat at the table, Peter was always making inappropriate comments, and Philip asked the dumbest questions. They talked when they should have listened, kept away the people they should have brought to Jesus, and woke him up when what he really needed was a good night's rest. ("Hey, Jesus, how about a little help? We're drowning over here.") Despite all this, Jesus never kicked any of them out of the group. Even when Judas committed the ultimate sin, when he sold the life of the Son of God for thirty pieces of silver, Jesus did not punish him. He allowed Judas to come to their final meal and allowed him to leave on his own accord. Jesus often admonished the disciples, but he used their mistakes as opportunities for growth, and the bottom line was always grace and reconciliation.

The twenty-first chapter of John is a beautiful picture of how Jesus restores wayward sheep. Peter, after making bold proclamations of his undying commitment to Jesus and his cause, had publically rejected him in the hour of his greatest need. After his resurrection, Jesus had appeared to the disciples on several occasions and undoubtedly had spoken to Peter, but there was still a tear in the relationship. So Jesus took Peter for a walk on the beach and helped Peter understand his place in the kingdom. If the Son of God would delay his return to heaven for the sole purpose of restoring one wayward member to good standing, how far should I go to deal with the difficult sheep in my fold?

Playing the Mercy Card

James understood this message when he wrote, "Speak and act as those who are going to be judged by law that gives freedom, because judgment without mercy will be shown to anyone who has not been merciful. *Mercy triumphs over judgment!*" (James 2:12 – 13, emphasis added).

A young Christian recently told me that he thought the verse said, "Mercy trumps judgment." What a great way to put it.

One of my favorite games is Spades, a simple card game in which spades are always the trump suit. The most powerful card in the game is the ace of spades. Whoever has the ace of spades controls his own destiny, so I always like to hold it until the last moment. I smile mockingly to myself as my opponents sweat while trick after trick is played and the ace does not appear. As we hold fewer and fewer cards in our hands, I see the pressure building. "Who has the ace? Who controls my destiny?" I imagine the enemy thinking. One by one each of the lesser cards is played and my opponent begins to shake almost imperceptibly as it begins to dawn on him that he may have guessed wrong; that perhaps his partner's hand is empty. At last the final trick is played. One by one the cards are laid on the table. All eyes are on me as I nonchalantly flip the final card toward the table. It spins slowly in the air, landing softly on top of the pile. My opponent's fate is sealed by the ultimate trump card. I smile across the table at my partner, offer a weak word of consolation to the opposing team, and call out, "Next!" (You do *not* want to play Spades against me.)

How would things turn out differently the next time you face a discipline situation in your church if you go in holding the trump card of mercy? You set up the meeting, gather the facts, and face the situation head-on. You sit down with the member who is clearly in sin; you call in the person who is spreading false rumors or you have lunch with the elder who is playing politics in the church. You lay the facts on the table, humbly admitting your own mistakes but also pointing to the unmistakable truth that sin must be dealt with. And just when the offending member least expects it, you pull out the trump card; you toss mercy on the table. You promise to pray for him every day, you commit to work for reconciliation, and you express your brokenness over the pain that your sin and his sin have caused in the church. Rather than asking him to leave the church, you tell him that if he is willing to do the hard work of repentance and restitution, you will do everything in your power to see him triumph over sin. And you ask if he will pray for you as well. Then you realize that the sinful member sitting across from you is not your opponent but your partner. You have not beaten him by playing the mercy card; together you have triumphed over your common enemy. Satan has lost this game. Next!

Free Pass for Everyone?

That seems pretty gooey, doesn't it? Everyone gets a free pass, no one is disciplined, and no one is removed from the church. Well, I guess it depends on your viewpoint. First, it's obvious that certain situations require very strict discipline. When there is repeated sin that does not lead to repentance and causes damage to the body of Christ, the pastor's job is to protect the sheep.

Several years ago at Seacoast, we heard that a woman was attempting to wreak havoc in marriages in the church. She was flirting with married men and trying to lure them into compromising situations. Once she felt she had enough evidence, she would threaten to call their wives and destroy their marriages if they didn't give her money. This situation called for an obvious response: we asked her to leave the church and then had to work hard to repair the damage she had done. We met with the woman and asked her to help us understand what was going on. At the end of the conversation, we prayed with her and then asked her to leave the church. I have not seen her since that day. This was a clear case when the role of the shepherd is to protect the sheep.

I've dealt with other situations involving leaders who had inappropriate relationships with teenagers, ex-husbands who threatened their former wives, and volunteers who posed a threat to the safety of the children. In each of these cases, there was a lack of repentance and therefore no choice; the offending party had to leave the church. However, cases like these are rarer than many of us believe. In most instances there are two sides to the story, and often repentance and reconciliation are possible when mercy is the first response.

Family Ties

At Seacoast I have no trouble thinking of the church as a family; it seems as though half the people who come are my relatives. Seeing the church as a family changes how we approach church discipline. If we view the church as an organization or a business, we'll likely believe that we have to thin the herd occasionally. (One pastor's response when people left the church was, "Every healthy body needs a good bowel movement once in a while.") One bad apple can spoil the whole bunch, so we need to move Granny Smith along before she ruins the congregation.

On the other hand, seeing the church as a family puts things in a different light. It's amazing what we'll put up with from our own family. When my children were small, it's a wonder we didn't excommunicate them from the house. They walked around half dressed with appalling odors emanating from their diapers. If my neighbors had looked or smelled half as bad, I would have moved to another neighborhood. My kids never pay their fair share of the bills, they consistently eat the last Twinkie in the box, and they are always asking for money. They expect me to help them with their homework, go to their band concerts, and admire their artwork. The most I get in return is an occasional "Thanks, Dad," or a halfhearted hug on their way out the door with the keys to my car in their grubby little paws. They have lied to me ("I didn't eat the cookies"), stolen from me ("I didn't know I was supposed to bring you the change"), and gossiped about me to their friends ("You won't believe what my dad did yesterday!"). But I've never asked either of them to leave the family. We have had several "come to Dad" meetings through the years, but not once have I threatened to excommunicate them. In fact, the opposite is true. I love my children more than anything on earth. I discipline them and coach them and pray for them every day, but I never think about disowning them. They belong to me and I belong to them. We're a family.

That's why Jesus tolerated his disciples. They weren't just associates, acquaintances, or even friends; they were family. They let him down, they turned their backs on him, they broke his heart, but they never stopped being his family. He taught them, corrected them, and believed in them. Jesus changed the world through twelve very flawed men into whom he poured himself and on whom he never gave up. How do you see the people of your congregation — as family or as associates?

Effective Discipline

Much has been written on methods of effective church discipline, but let's take a look at four basic situations and ideas for handling each.

1. *When the offense is private and the offender repentant.* Recently I received a frantic email from a friend's wife who was at the end of her rope and didn't know where to turn. Her husband was not living up to his obligations to the family, was not paying the bills, and had begun drinking again after several years of sobriety. If she didn't see some change, she was going to leave him.

    I called a mutual friend and we set up a meeting. We confronted the husband with the situation as we understood it and asked to hear his side of the story. After a long, passionate conversation, he admitted that he was headed in the wrong direction and wanted to find his way back. We helped him outline several steps to recover his sobriety and restore his marriage and prayed with him for wisdom for the future. He returned home and began rebuilding his marriage and his life. We continue to check in with him and his wife on a regular basis, and they are making great progress.

Many, if not most, situations like this are best handled one-on-one or at the small group level. Small groups facilitate accountability and understanding. People are vested in each other's lives and can help in the restorative process.

2. *When the offense is private and the sinner unrepentant.* What if the husband in this situation had refused to admit a problem or to repent of his sin? In Matthew 18 Jesus gives clear instructions on dealing with an unrepentant offender. Again the process begins with a one-on-one confrontation and is best dealt with at the lowest level possible. The goal does not change: repentance, reconciliation, and restoration.

3. *When the offense is public and the offender repentant.* Sometimes, however, sin is so public and impacts so many people that it has to be handled in a public manner. A few years ago a very talented leader at Seacoast was caught in a very public sin. He knew he had sinned, and his heart was broken over the damage he had done. He came forward and confessed his sin to our senior pastor and immediately expressed his desire to do whatever it took to restore the trust that had been placed in him and to repair the relationships and young lives that were impacted.

    After consulting with the leadership team, our senior pastor went to a meeting of the group that this leader oversaw. He had the young man come forward at the end of the meeting and confess his sin to the crowd. He expressed his sorrow and tearfully asked for forgiveness from those he had hurt. He was then asked to step down from any leadership position for six months. Over that period of time, he continued to work behind the scenes at the church. At the end of six months, he was publically restored to a position of leadership.

Today he is a happily married father and continues to grow in maturity and in influence.

When a sin or offense in a leader's life impacts a large group of people, the discipline has to be handled in a public manner. If, however, grace is applied through reasoned punishment, a level of maturity in the leader and the congregation can be reached that might not be achieved in any other way.

4. *When the offense is public and the offender unrepentant.* The most difficult situation is when the offense is public and there is no repentance. A few years ago we had to confront a talented and charismatic leader. Since committing his life to Christ at Seacoast, he had brought many of his friends to the church, served on our worship team, and volunteered in the youth ministry. We discovered that he was involved in an inappropriate relationship with a teenage girl at the church. Despite indisputable evidence, he refused to admit his sin and repent. After a long process in which he was confronted one-on-one, then by a group of leaders, and finally in front of the leadership team, he was asked to leave the church.

When we ask someone to leave the church, it's important that we share our decision appropriately. If the congregant is not someone known to the greater church body, there is no reason to discuss the dismissal publically; it will only bring confusion. We do need to share with those who have a connection with the offending member. If the individual is known to the entire church, we must explain publically the decision to ask this person to leave. The offense should be outlined in general terms and the process that led to dismissal explained. All questions should be handled privately. Answers should be given when appropriate, but we are not called to simply satisfy the curious.

Mishandling church discipline issues will not only keep your church from growing; it can destroy the health of your congregation. I planted a rosebush in our yard as a gift for my wife several years ago, but I haven't touched it since. It has long branches with menacing thorns that threaten to draw blood every time someone comes near. While the bush still produces a few roses every year, it is actually a dangerous eyesore. I would just dig it up, but it has sentimental value to my wife. What my wayward rosebush needs is a good pruning, but I don't know how to trim the branches and not kill the roots. The thorn in the flesh at your church needs the same kind of pruning — discipline that promotes life rather than death.

To get greater insight into how to walk the tightrope of discipline and restoration, I went to my friend from Baton Rouge, Louisiana, Dino Rizzo. Dino's years of practical experience in dealing with difficult people give him a valuable perspective on this sticky question.

················· **SPOTLIGHT** ·················

Dino Rizzo, Healing Place Church

About thirty pastors were crammed into a dingy Sunday school classroom in an old church located in a suburb outside of Atlanta. It was the first meeting of what would become the Association of Related Churches, a church-planting organization founded by Seacoast along with several other churches. Officially I was there to represent Seacoast, but my real reason for coming was to hear Dino Rizzo. I had heard a great deal about the former surfer who had built "a healing place for a hurting world" among the down-and-out in Baton Rouge, Louisiana. Dino was supposed to be a funny, outrageous, and powerful communicator who spoke with intense passion. I scanned the crowd wondering if Dino was one of the stereotypical preachers in cheap suits and garish ties, the GQ model in the perfectly matched polo and khakis, or the laid back rock star in the untucked shirt and blue jeans. I never suspected Dino was the guy in the ski hat and sweatshirt slouched in the corner, fighting the flu and a really bad haircut. When Dino's turn to speak came, I thought, "You have got to be kidding me! Can any good thing come out of the bayou?"

And then Dino began to tell the story of how God had led him in 1993 to a mostly abandoned church building on the bad side of Baton Rouge to build a ministry for the people no one else cared about. Over the next forty-five minutes, I laughed, I cried, and I was challenged to the core. Dino's passion for lost and hurting people colors everything he does, and that passion flows out through the staff and members of Healing Place Church. From its very humble beginnings with a handful of people in a broken-down building, HPC now has four campuses and ministers to more than five thousand people every weekend. The church is making a tremendous impact not only in Baton Rouge and Louisiana, but all around the world. Over the past several years since I first met Dino, I have come to respect him as one of the most grace-filled pastors I have ever known. I knew Dino would have great insight into the balance between grace and discipline.

How do you balance being full of grace and maintaining church discipline?

I would have to say this has been a progressive walk for me as I have continued on my own journey of a balanced life of grace and truth, discipline and redemption, judgment and mercy. God is a God of divine order, so that has to happen without a doubt. But I believe there is a life-giving way to operate when the kingdom priorities and principles are maintained and lives are being valued and encouraged. At the end of the day, I have to be fully alive to my own need for grace. I can then lead and operate in it toward others so that Healing Place has God's full blessings and sets biblical boundaries.

Have you experienced a time when someone who was disciplined in your church was later restored to the body? What lessons did you learn in the process?

Most definitely — I have seen it several times. When you have passion to be a healing place for a hurting world, God sends the gift of hurting people. We all know that people who are hurting can hurt others. When we have to step in to serve in those toxic moments, it is for redemption first. We are also called, however, to guard the flock that he has called us to serve. Those conversations can become life-giving confrontations; I have seen people repent in my office, or at an altar, or even supernaturally during the Lord's Supper. But I have also seen some walk away from the church after being confronted; too much pride and ego. As a pastor you have to watch over the flock and speak the truth in love. One of the most amazing things, though, is to just sit down with someone who is hurting others, just two chairs in a room, and see the Spirit of Christ salvage things. Pretty cool stuff to see. I think that would be a biblical model, come to think of it.

Have you seen other pastors make mistakes in the area of church discipline?

There was a time in our area of the country that it seemed, sad to say, that the prevailing attitude among pastors was that the harder the discipline the better. There was some sort of weird win to those who really knew how to slam people, how to put others in their place. The mind-set was kind of a "Don't let the door hit you on your way out" approach to church discipline. I am all in favor of not allowing or tolerating outright discord or sin or rebellion, but I believe you can be kind, nice, strong, sensitive, respectful, and bold all in the same environment. I believe that was the atmosphere of Jesus — meek but in no way weak.

What is your response to the statement "It is better to err on the side of grace"?

I would be very down with it. I believe compassion has to be our starting point even in the adversarial moments, especially if you understand the compassion of restoration. I always try to remind our staff to ask, "How can this situation be redemptive, bring restoration, and glorify Christ? Let's give it all we have." The person or persons who have been hurt or caused the hurt have to choose how they will respond, because they are grown-ups and this is a volunteer sport.

What would you say to the pastor of a smaller congregation who is dealing with a sensitive issue that seems to require church discipline?

Don't go it alone. Always find someone who can help put a shoulder underneath the load and help carry some of it. Church problems can be nauseating, so you've got to get some relief. I always involve another brother or sister who is a spiritual-thinking person to assist. I'm just not that smart to go it all by myself.

IQ Test

Think through the following questions on your own. If you feel you need to grow in this area, find another pastor who will meet with you and discuss your answers.

1. How do you see the people of your congregation — as family or as associates?

2. Do you tend to err on the side of mercy or justice in dealing with difficult people in your church?

3. When was the last time you asked someone to leave your church? Do you feel you handled the situation properly? Could the situation have been handled in a way that the

individual would not have had to leave? What would you do differently next time?

4. Is there currently a situation in your church that needs to be confronted? Why do you feel it needs to be addressed? Who can help you walk through this confrontation?

5. Is there someone you have confronted in the past to whom you need to reach out? How will you open that conversation?

9

MIXING MINISTRY AND BUSINESS

"I'D LIKE TO OFFER YOU THE BREAD, THE WINE,
AND AN EXCELLENT INVESTMENT OPPORTUNITY."

Have you ever had this conversation? "Pastor, I know the ministry doesn't pay very well and that you want to make sure your family's needs are taken care of. I want to offer you an incredible opportunity that could change your life. For a very small investment of time and money, you can supplement the income you receive from the church, secure your family's financial future, and provide a great product to the members of your congregation." You are then given a chance to sell soap, long-distance service, travel websites, or a variety of other can't-miss products and investment opportunities.

The first time I heard of this type of business, I was in elementary school and a couple of men in my dad's church came over to the house to pitch him the chance of a lifetime. Their product was a soda fountain you put in the trunk of your car. While driving down the highway, you could pop open your glove compartment and dispense a cup of your favorite cold beverage. The men were sure that most of the people in my dad's church would jump at the chance to own one of these marvelous new machines, and the best part was that my dad would get a percentage of the profit on every unit sold to his members. I was stunned when my dad turned them down. (Cold soda in the car anytime I wanted it? That was the coolest thing my ten-year-old mind could imagine. My forty-six-year-old mind is still pretty intrigued with the possibility.) My dad thanked them for their time but told them he could not take advantage of his position as pastor to make money off of his church members. Over the years I heard my dad turn down many seemingly lucrative opportunities because he didn't want to compromise the integrity of the office of pastor.

Mixing business and pastoring is a tricky proposition at best. When does it make sense for a pastor to work at an outside job? When is he crossing the line by using his influence as a pastor to build his personal business? This is one of the stupid mistakes that I made in spectacular fashion.

A Tale of Two Business Adventures

It seemed like a good idea at the time. My wife and I were pastoring Church on the Lake, which had a total budget of $65,000 per year.

That covered my salary, all of the building costs, ministry costs, and gas for the church's lawn mower; needless to say, things were tight. When Pat, a business owner in the church who was somewhere between a seeker and a true follower of Christ, offered me a job working in his computer store, it sounded like an answer to prayer. The job would give my family some much-needed cash, I'd always enjoyed working with computers, and I would have the opportunity to disciple a new believer daily. I agreed to go to work part-time building and repairing computers as well as working on the sales floor.

For the next several months, I left the church each day at 3:00 p.m. to go work at the computer store for a couple of hours, as well as a few hours most Saturdays. I learned a lot about repairing computers, I met many people in the community I never would have met if I hadn't worked at the store, and I was able to spend a great deal of time talking with Pat about his spiritual journey. At the time it seemed like a good situation; looking back several years later, I realized it was one of the stupidest mistakes I have made in ministry. Let's look at a few of the problems:

1. I went to work for a man I was trying to disciple. Pat had some ethical challenges and repeatedly put me in situations that were questionable at best. There were often questions that I needed to answer as his pastor, but I was in the role of his employee.

2. Other leaders in the church felt Pat had more influence than he should have. He wasn't really a believer yet, but he had more input on the direction of the church than anyone.

3. The community saw me as a salesman and repairman rather than a pastor. PC Place became the face of Church on the Lake in our community and the impression we left was not always positive. It's okay if the gospel is offensive; it's not okay if the used computer you bought from the pastor is offensive. I am convinced there are people I was not able to share Jesus with because I had sold them a bad computer.

4. At a time when I should have been focusing on my family and
    ministry, I was spending a significant amount of time hawk-
    ing computers. I had a growing young church, in addition to
    a wife and two young children; I lost precious time with each
    that I will never get back.

After I'd spent a few months working for Pat in his store, it
dawned on me that this setup wasn't a good idea. I finally left the
computer business and went back to being a full-time husband, father, and pastor. We missed the additional income, but God took care
of our needs.

I recently had another chance to work a second job while being in
full-time ministry. Greg Ligon of Leadership Network contacted Seacoast and asked for permission to talk with me about filling a part-
time role with LN. Our senior pastor felt we could work it out if they
offered me a job. When the offer eventually came, I discussed it with
the leadership team at the church before accepting the position. We
worked out a modification to my salary at Seacoast to compensate for
the time I would spend working on LN projects. We talked through
possible conflicts of interest, and everyone agreed that this could be a
good opportunity for me personally as well as for Seacoast. I accepted
the job offer and worked for both Seacoast and LN for about two and
a half years. I recently left the position at LN to take on a bigger role
at Seacoast (and to have enough margin in my life to write this book),
but having both jobs turned out to be positive experience.

Through my own stupidity and experience, I have learned that
there is a right way and a wrong way for a pastor to approach working
outside of his church. My job in the computer business was detri-
mental to my church and my family, while my time with Leadership
Network was a growth opportunity for Seacoast and for me. Let's
take a look at the keys to making an outside business opportunity a
positive experience for your ministry.

How Should I Approach Outside Business Opportunities?

Bivocational pastors go back to the apostle Paul, who continued his work as a tentmaker while spreading the gospel to the Gentiles and writing most of the New Testament. Luke seemed to continue in his vocation as a physician as he worked side by side with Paul. Many of the pastors I admire the most work in more than one arena. There are, however, some real pitfalls to trying to balance the call to pastoral ministry and the demands of working another job. Let's look at a list of dos and don'ts of bivocational ministry.

The Dos of a Second Income

Do reject the myth that to be a pastor you have to be poor. Nothing is more virtuous about a pastor who has little than about a pastor who has a lot. I have met bitter, angry, arrogant, poor pastors, and I have met humble, open, generous pastors who are wealthy in comparison. God wants your needs to be taken care of, and in taking care of your needs, he may choose to bless you with material wealth. Pursuing additional income to secure your family's future doesn't mean compromising the integrity of the ministry; what opportunities you pursue and how you pursue them are the keys.

Do celebrate the opportunities that God may bring your way. I believe that every opportunity that comes my way should be examined. Some opportunities are easy to discard — for instance, a side job dealing blackjack at the local casino probably isn't a good idea. Other opportunities, however, might be God's way of providing for my family. When Paul discovered Aquila and Priscilla were tentmakers (Acts 18), he decided to stay with them and join them in their business. He realized that God had opened a door to take care of his physical needs.

Do remember that opportunity can be temptation in disguise. As Seacoast Church gained the reputation around the country as one of the leading churches in the multisite movement, more and more opportunities began to come my way. I had the chance to speak at conferences, to consult with churches, and to contribute to magazine articles — all good things that I enjoy doing. I shared with a wise mentor all of the intriguing doors that seemed to be opening at the same time. As he sat back in his chair contemplating my amazing life, I saw a grin begin to form. "Well, you know," he finally said, "opportunity is often temptation in disguise." Suddenly my amazing life didn't seem so amazing, because I knew he was right. (He usually is.) I am seldom tempted to knock over the local mini-mart or to kill my neighbor and boil his body in a vat of bleach. I am often tempted, however, to squander my limited time on many activities and never really focus on the one thing God has called me to.

No matter how good an opportunity looks, always analyze it in light of what God has called you to accomplish as well all the other good stuff you are already doing. I'm finding that a good opportunity filter for me is to ask, "What am I going to stop doing so that I can start doing this?" For instance, to have time to write this book, I have given up eating and sleeping. (Actually, I'm writing the book on vacation time I have accumulated at Seacoast with the full support of my church, my wife, and my family.) Is that can't-miss opportunity a blessing or a temptation?

Do be transparent with the church leadership about your outside business ventures. One of the lessons I learned from my dad about ministry is that if I'm doing something that I don't want others in the church to know about, I probably shouldn't be doing it in the first place. Whether you are investing in real estate, speaking at conferences, or selling paintings of poker-playing dogs on eBay, the leadership team at your church should be informed of what you are doing. One of the biggest mistakes pastors make in this area is trying to hide their business ventures from their leadership team. They will eventually hear about what you are doing; it's best if you are the one who tells them.

The Don'ts of a Second Income

Don't go into business with a church member. I'm sure there are cases in which being in business with a church member works, but it is still a bad idea. A business partnership compromises the pastor-parishioner relationship. Your congregation needs a spiritual leader who can speak the truth in love regardless of the condition of the real estate market or the way sales are going. There will always be opportunities to go into business or form a partnership with someone in the congregation, but it will never be a good idea.

Don't use church time, property, or employees to further your business. This is a tricky issue, but the bottom line is just don't do it. When you talk with your board about the outside business you are entering, you and the board need to agree on very specific boundaries and stick with them. You need to work on the business before or after the time you spend in the church office. You need to hire someone other than your assistant at the church to handle the administrative work of the outside business. You need a very explicit understanding with the church before you use a church computer, church software, or any other church property in the pursuit of outside interests.

This area is a major test of integrity. When balancing church work with secular work, you'll be tempted to blur the lines: What could it hurt to run a few copies for the business on the church copy machine? A couple of long-distance calls won't break the bank. I need to get a bill sent off today and I don't have a stamp or the time to run to the post office. I once worked on staff with a guy who constantly blurred these lines. He would use church time and equipment to do work on other projects, and he would occasionally use the church credit card for personal purchases and reimburse the church later. He was eventually caught remodeling his house with materials purchased on the church account at the hardware store. That's a slippery slope you don't want to risk sliding down.

Don't use church members as your prospect list. Many pastors have fallen prey to the lure of easy money through multilevel marketing. The pitch is similar regardless of the product being offered. Your congregation is already buying soap, magazines, or long distance, so why shouldn't the church (and you) make some income off those sales? The question is, what do you give up in order to make a little profit?

Your church database is every multilevel marketer's dream; they would give almost anything to have access to those names. They fantasize about a sales letter with your name at the bottom personally addressed to everyone who attends your church, giving them the opportunity of a lifetime to get in on the ground floor of an incredible investment. Those names, however, have been entrusted to you by God. They represent lives he has placed in your path to care for, to disciple, and to protect. Selling helpful products, secular or sacred, is not a sin; using your flock to make those sales is.

Don't allow business to hinder ministry or harm your family. As pastors, we need to hold any business ventures we're involved in very loosely. Are you ready to walk away from the business if there is a hint that it is inhibiting in any way what God wants to do through your church? I don't believe there is a higher calling or a greater privilege than being allowed to pastor God's people, and everything else in my life, other than my family, should be subordinate to that calling. Ask the leaders in your church if they feel that business is hindering your ministry. Ask your family members if they are comfortable with the time you are spending away from them.

What If I'm Really Good at Business?

My friend had been in ministry almost all of his adult life. He grew up in a pastor's home and, despite a vow never to become a pastor, ended up working for his dad as a youth pastor. After several years of success in youth ministry, he felt the tug to plant a new church. With the blessing of his father and the backing of his home church, he launched out on his own. The church did well, but in the midst of pastoring the church, he had the opportunity to supplement his income by working in the marketplace. He didn't solicit clients in his congregation and worked hard to balance his time and attention between his business and his church. The business did very well, and soon he was making more money from the marketplace than he was from the church. He began to look forward to the day when he could work for the church for free and earn all of his income from business.

Eventually, however, he realized something wasn't right. He loved working with clients, seeing them succeed because of the help he was able to give them. On the other hand, he was just going through the motions at the church. He didn't enjoy ministry and didn't feel particularly gifted as a pastor. He came to the realization that God had not wired him to be a pastor; he had gone that direction because it just seemed like the right thing to do. He shared his feelings with a few close friends and began to work with the church to find his successor. Today the church he started is doing well with a pastor who feels called and gifted to full-time ministry. My friend is working full-time in the marketplace, supporting the ministry he once worked in and fulfilling the plan God has for his life.

Not everyone who is good at business should leave the ministry, but it's very important to know why you are doing what you do. I've been told that the only reason to become a pastor is because you can't do anything else. To the contrary, you should sense deep inside your spirit that being a pastor is what you were made to do. This calling doesn't preclude earning money from other sources, but it does prohibit being a pastor as a sideline. Although Paul was a tentmaker, he always described himself as an apostle of Christ. Clearly, in Paul's mind, "apostle" was his identity; tent making was just a side job.

Someone who has really figured out the balance between business and ministry is my friend Dr. Ron Hamilton. Ron is both a pastor and a dentist, so I knew he could give us some valuable insight.

···················· **SPOTLIGHT** ····················

Dr. Ron Hamilton, Seacoast Church, West Ashley Campus

Dr. Ron Hamilton is the campus pastor of Seacoast's West Ashley, South Carolina, campus and my dentist. (When Ron says getting people to volunteer in children's ministry is like pulling teeth, he knows exactly what he is talking about.) We've had several discussions about his campus while I was in the chair waiting for my mouth to numb up. It's amazing how much more smoothly budget negotiations go during a root canal.

Ron is one of the highest-capacity leaders I have ever worked with. While he was building his dental practice, he was also helping build one of the most successful youth ministries in Charleston before helping start Seacoast in 1988. Since 2002, when the West Ashley campus began, Ron has seen his congregation grow to more than one thousand attendees every weekend. He continues to oversee a large paid and volunteer staff, serve on the Seacoast management team, and work as a dentist. I knew that Ron could help us understand how to navigate the difficult waters of maintaining a business and a ministry.

How did you come to the decision to remain in dentistry and pastor a congregation?

God has allowed me to be involved in dentistry and ministry since 1980. That year that I started my dental practice, I helped start a youth ministry that grew to over three hundred students, and our daughter was born. I learned quickly how to minister through teams and the value of mentoring other leaders. Basically I knew if I didn't mentor others, I was toast! After four years assisting the youth pastor at our church, he asked me to take over for him when he left to start a church out of town. I prayed, met with the pastors of the church, and sought out whether I should quit the dentistry and go full-time. They wisely counseled me not to quit dentistry — that God had called me to be a dentist also, and that God was still using me there with other dentists and in mission work. So I learned even more how to work through other people, nurture leaders, and build teams. I did that for two years until I stepped out of that position in 1986 and in early 1987 started meeting with Greg Surratt to dream and plan to launch Seacoast. I learned to delegate and build teams and care for leaders by being in the fire, but it has been a great training time in my life that has helped me for years.

When I started the West Ashley campus of Seacoast, I knew it was time to sell the practice so that I would not have any administration involvement in dentistry. I have always felt that God gave me dentistry as a ministry, so I discussed with Pastor Greg the best approach. He confirmed the sense I had that God had led me to dentistry and that I would always have a hand in it — no pun intended. When we started the West Ashley campus, I sold the practice but continued working one day a week in dentistry. Since then the ministry I have in dentistry has been confirmed time and time again as I am called to minister to other dentists and their staffs. I also am able to keep my license and perform mission work in dentistry as I did recently in Honduras.

How do you balance pastoring a church and working as a dentist?

The key is keeping your focus on your gifts and what God has called you to do. My gifts are leadership, carrying the Seacoast vision God has given us, and building strong teams to carry out the vision. I do not have any management duties at the dentist office, so the one day a week I work in dentistry does not carry over at all into what I do in the ministry. I also have email at work so I stay connected throughout the day.

For me the balance comes in the gifting I have been given and being trained early in my situation to mentor leaders and build teams. The reality is that at times I am not in balance when ministry situations come that require extra time and effort, but sleep is overrated, and we will rest in heaven, right?

Have you ever faced a conflict of interest between the two?

The only conflict has been some meetings that were scheduled on the day I do dentistry, but they normally work out and it is rare when it doesn't. I also use lunch that day to schedule meetings with people over ministry issues.

What mistakes have you seen other pastors make who are involved in businesses outside their own church?

Most of the mistakes would flow out of both positions requiring a lot of leadership and administration and trying to do both. For me the dentistry has been set up so I have no management or administration duties. My attention and energy are directed to the ministry fully, and having a high energy level helps! As most of us know, ministry is 24-7, so pacing yourself is key. And, again, doing the behind-the-scenes work on developing people on your team is the key.

What advice would you give to a pastor who is considering working in another area as well?

First, pray about it a lot and have godly, respected people help you look at it. Some people are single-focused people, while others are more multitask-oriented. Know yourself and the abilities God has given you, and have people take a look with you to give you the perspective you need. It also helps to have a track record of being able to train leaders and delegate to help you manage your time. It would be tough to have to do that cold turkey without a gradual growth time in being able to manage your time and resources.

IQ Test

If you are currently bivocational or are considering entering a business venture in addition to the ministry you are currently paid to do, answer the following questions with a trusted friend.

1. What advantages do you see in pursuing a second job or an outside business interest? What pitfalls do you see?

2. What safeguards will you have in place to guard against a conflict of interest between your business and your ministry? Who will hold you accountable for your time and resources?

3. How does your family feel about your taking on additional responsibilities? How does the church leadership feel about it?

4. Do you see your second job or business venture as a short-term solution or a long-term commitment?

5. Is God calling you out of vocational ministry and into the marketplace? Could you better serve the kingdom using your talents and abilities in the business world and volunteering in ministry?

10

LETTING COMMITTEES
STEER THE SHIP

"I WANTED 60-WATT INSTEAD OF 40-WATT BULBS,
BUT THE WORSHIP ILLUMINATION COMMITTEE SAID NO."

Toward the end of my son's senior year in high school, my wife and I were invited to serve on the parents' graduation party planning committee. I never actually saw the invitation, but my wife assured me that both parents were required to attend. I tend to avoid events that combine the words "committee" and "planning," but I couldn't find a way out this time. We arrived fashionably late (I might have been dragging my feet) to the school cafeteria, where we found a small group of concerned parents huddled around a lunch table deep into a very serious discussion. I assumed they were hashing out an important topic like providing chaperones to curb the hormones of the emancipated teenagers, hiring taste testers to ensure the punch remained alcohol-free throughout the evening, or selecting the right band for the dance. (I was hoping they'd get the Eagles, but it seemed like a long shot.) After brief introductions ("Mike's parents, meet David's parents"), we were brought up to speed on the crisis of the moment: What color napkins to buy? I shot my wife a "You've got to be kidding me" look, and she returned a "Keep your mouth shut and continue smiling like the goober you are" look. For the next forty-five minutes we weighed the pros and cons of blue, white, or black napkins. I made a motion that we let the students wipe their mouths on their sleeves, but no one seconded it. I don't remember the outcome of this fascinating debate; I eventually started counting ceiling tiles and wondering how many people we could seat in the cafeteria if it was a church.

Finally, the committee decided to adjourn for the evening and finish the planning at the next meeting. My wife and I said goodbye to all the parents whose children's names we couldn't remember, and as we returned to our car, Sherry whispered, "That's two hours of my life I'll never get back." We agreed that we would pay whatever fine the committee levied, but we wouldn't be attending any more meetings. A couple of months later, the party came off well (although the Eagles weren't able to make it), the punch was alcohol-free, and the seniors stayed pure — well, at least as pure as when they arrived. I think the napkins were blue, or maybe they were checked. The other

parents were cordial, but I think they resented us for escaping committee purgatory when they had not.

Unfortunately, many churches are run like a graduation party
planning committee. Rather than focusing on expanding the kingdom and growing disciples, these churches hold meeting after meeting to endlessly rehash trivia. Ill-equipped board members engage in
political infighting and turf wars while God-given opportunities are
missed and the church remains stagnant.

Sometime in the history of the American church, it was decided
that the church could best be led by committee. I don't know if this
decision was made after a motion was seconded and voted on or
when an exhausted pastor just gave up, but committees and boards
dominate the life of many churches across the country. Properly led
and in right relationship to the pastor and the vision of the church,
these teams can be instrumental in fulfilling the God-given mission
of the local congregation. When one of these groups, however, is out
of alignment, it can bring a church to a screeching halt.

Clearly team-based ministry is a very effective biblical model of
leadership. As we discussed in chapter 1, Moses' father-in-law helped
him set up a well-defined team to lead the children of Israel in the
desert. One of the first things Jesus did in ministry was to form his
team. Everywhere the apostle Paul went, he took a team with him.
The challenge of working in teams or committees comes when the
lines of leadership become blurred.

Every effective team has a strong leader. When the Chicago Bulls
won six NBA championships, there was no question that Michael
Jordan was the court leader. When the 1980 USA hockey team pulled
off the Miracle on Ice, everyone knew that coach Herb Brooks was in
charge. When the Indianapolis Colts won their first Super Bowl in
2007, Tony Dungy was the undisputed guide. A team without a clear
leader is like a boat without a rudder; a rudderless boat may arrive
at port, but it will take a long time to get there and will endanger everyone on board in the process. A church led by committees, boards,
or teams that are not submitted to God's anointed leader will lurch

from one project to the next and from one pastor to the next but will seldom accomplish much for the kingdom of God.

The key to effective team-based ministry is to remember that leaders lead and teams follow. When teams lead, you have chaos; when leaders follow, you have confusion. Imagine Tony Dungee walking into the Indianapolis locker room and asking if anyone has a game plan for their next game against the New England Patriots.

"Guys, I don't have a clue how to handle Tom Brady and the Patriots' offense, so I thought we'd form some cross-functional teams to work on our playbook. Let's get the quarterbacks, linebackers, and locker room attendants to create a defensive scheme, and let's have the running backs, defensive linemen, and announcing crew work on our offense. I'll work with everyone else to put together a plan for the post-game celebration. We have some serious napkin questions to address."

If God has called you to lead your church, then it is very important that you step up and lead. The role of pastor isn't a license to be a dictator or to ignore the input of valued counselors, but there are some questions that only you have enough information to answer. No one else knows what you do about the vision God has given you for the church. No one else has the experience you have at leading the congregation. And no one else has the big picture of the entire ministry of the church that you have. Everyone has a piece of the picture, but you as the pastor are the ultimate keeper of the vision.

I had the chance this year to tour St. Paul's Cathedral in London. Standing beneath the massive dome and seeing the incredible artwork 280 feet above was a very moving experience. It was obvious that St. Paul's was built with a singular vision. I learned that when the great English architect Christopher Wren began to build St. Paul's, he employed the gifts and talents of the best artists, masons, and painters in the kingdom to assist in the construction of his masterpiece. Over the thirty-five years it took to build the cathedral, many of these artisans came and went, as did the monarchs who ruled England, but Wren's vision never wavered. While the dome was being built, Wren, who by this time was more than seventy years old, was hauled up over 280 feet to the top of the dome in a basket at least once a week to inspect the progress. The magnificent church was built by a team, but the world still knows that Christopher Wren was the leader because St. Paul's was his vision.

St. Paul's namesake, the apostle Paul, had a crisis of team-based management on his last trip to Jerusalem, as recorded by his team-mate Luke in Acts 21:

> After we had been there for some time, a prophet named Agabus arrived from Judea. He came to us and borrowed Paul's belt and used it to tie his own hands and feet. He said, "The Holy Spirit says, 'This is how the Jews in Jerusalem will tie up the man who wears this belt. Then they will give him to the older leaders.'"
>
> When we all heard this, we and the people there begged Paul not to go to Jerusalem. But he said, "Why are you crying and making me so sad? I am not only ready to be tied up in Jerusalem, I am ready to die for the Lord Jesus!"
>
> We could not persuade him to stay away from Jerusalem. So we stopped begging him and said, "We pray that what the Lord wants will be done." (vv. 10 – 14 NCV)

Paul listened to the input of his team and knew that what they said was true, but he also knew God had a bigger vision for his life. Like Christopher Wren, Paul had a view that not even his most committed follower possessed. Imagine how different the world would be if Paul had followed rather than led his team. Would Paul ever have made it to Rome? Would we have the Prison Epistles? When leaders do not lead, the consequences are far-reaching.

The Art of Teamwork

Get a Vision

So how do you lead in a team-based (committee-based, board-based) environment? The most important key is to make sure you have a clear vision of what God has called you to do. This step may seem obvious, but most of us can probably point to times in our lives when we said we were leading from a God-given vision when we were really working on a personal agenda. Do you know that you know that you know that God has called you to a specific mission at a specific place at a specific time? If not, you do not have a committee problem; you have a vision problem. The first step for you is to get away and find God. God gave this promise to Moses: "But if from there you seek the LORD your God, you will find him if you look for him with all your heart and with all your soul" (Deut. 4:29).

If you do not have a clear, gut-wrenching, God-sized vision for what God wants to do through your church, it's time to seek the Lord your God with all your heart and soul. At times in my ministry I have lain facedown on the carpet and refused to get up until I heard from God. It's amazing how a good carpet burn can bring clarity to a situation. Don't try to lead until you get that clarity from heaven.

Vision is the key to leading any team. People will not follow policies and procedures or carefully planned agendas; people want to follow a compelling vision. When the people begged Paul not to return to Jerusalem, he painted a vision of being ready to lay down his life for Jesus. While his team was sad that this journey might be the end, they could see that Paul had a clear mission, a clear vision from God. As Christopher Wren led a team of artists and builders for thirty-five years while constructing St. Paul's Cathedral, he returned again and again to the original vision he had sketched for King Charles II. As Herb Overstreet pushed his young hockey team beyond what they thought they could endure, he never let them forget the near impossible vision of winning the Olympic gold medal. A confident leader with a compelling vision will take a team to places they could never get to on their own.

Share the Dream

The vision at Seacoast Church from day one has been to help people become fully devoted followers of Christ, but recently we have seen that an important component of that vision is for each member to create and follow an individualized written spiritual growth plan. (For more information see www.mynextsteps.org.)

The challenge with this new vision was how to share it. We could print a new brochure, we could preach a sermon series on spiritual growth, or we could put up billboards around town urging people to check out MyLameSpiritualLife.com. In the end we decided to just start with our key leaders. We knew our campus pastors had to have buy-in before they would share the new vision with the members. Rather than trying to implement a new churchwide program, we began by introducing the concept at a retreat for all of the campus pastors. We painted a picture of the power of each member of our church working on an individual plan of spiritual growth. We then asked the pastors to help create a template for a plan that everyone could use. Finally, we each created our own plan and tried the concept in our own lives for three months. The end result was a leadership team fired up about a new direction for our church rather than a reluctant team of foot draggers.

Define the Mission

Once your team understands and buys into the vision, it's time to define the mission. What specific role does this team play in the overall vision of the church? Each team, committee, or board needs to understand its piece of the mission. Without a clearly defined mission, team members begin to drift into areas where their input isn't really needed.

A good example of a team with a well-defined mission is the board of trustees at Seacoast. The board is responsible for overseeing all long-term debt, obligations, and building projects at Seacoast. Its responsibility encompasses 30 percent of the overall budget of the church. It is not responsible for the quality of the youth ministry, the length of the sermons, or the color of the paint in the foyer. The board does an excellent job of overseeing the budget and isn't distracted by wandering down paths it has no need to explore.

In defining the mission of a team, it's vital to include the members in the process. An important principle I learned from the Dale Carnegie Leadership organization is that people will support a world they help create. Your board will support the mission that you create together. One of the best ways to empower a board or committee is to take some extended time to define why the team exists and what its primary mission is. First, recast the vision for the church; why does the church exist? Next, brainstorm all of the ways the team can be a part of that vision. Then narrow the list of possible ideas down to four or five core areas where the team can focus its energy. Finally, create a tightly defined, clearly understood mission for the team. At future meetings of the team, revisit this definition frequently so that everyone stays on board and on track with the team's mission.

Empower the Missionaries

Once your teams understand the vision of the church and have a well-defined mission, it's time to turn them loose to lead. If you have strong leaders who are committed to the vision and mission, the team will accomplish far more than you could ever accomplish on your own. Teams and boards that are well led and loosely held can be an indomitable force. Teams that are weakly led and tightly controlled will be an endless source of headaches and confusion. The pastor's job is to keep the vision fresh, the team on mission, and the path clear. The team's job is to accomplish the mission.

Getting the Board on Board

Implementing change in a church that has been led by committees rather than vision is difficult but not impossible. It requires a new vision from God and a complete commitment to that vision. Change will involve a lot of honest conversation, a willingness to face misunderstanding and animosity, and an unwavering commitment to the task at hand. When Nehemiah considered the task of rebuilding the crumbled wall that had once surrounded Jerusalem, the job seemed impossible. He was underfunded, undersupplied, and under-manned. But he had a vision from God to restore the city to its former place of prominence by rebuilding what the enemy had destroyed. He called the people of the city together and challenged them: "Then I said to them, 'You see the trouble we are in: Jerusalem lies in ruins, and its gates have been burned with fire. Come, let us rebuild the wall of Jerusalem, and we will no longer be in disgrace'" (Neh. 2:17).

Despite extreme opposition and seemingly insurmountable odds, Nehemiah was able to rebuild the entire wall in only fifty-two days by leading from vision and keeping the teams on mission. Are you ready to rebuild the walls of the congregation God has entrusted to you?

Dave Browning, founding pastor of Christ the King Community Church based in Mount Vernon, Washington, is a revolutionary pastor who is changing the definition of church in America and beyond. I recently picked Dave's brain on how he works in a team environment.

· · · · · · · · · · · · · · · · · · ·**SPOTLIGHT**· · · · · · · · · · · · · · · · · · · ·

Dave Browning, Christ the King Community Church

The first time I met Dave Browning I knew he was a dangerous man. We were sitting around a table at a Leadership Network Leadership Community for multisite churches discussing this new idea of becoming one church in many locations. Everyone else at the table was a leader at a huge influential church. I felt as out of place as a Calvinist at a Pentecostal tent revival. The specific topic was what ministries need to be replicated at every campus of a multiple-location church. The first leader said that after extensive study and a great deal of discussion by the elders, his church had reduced the number of essential ministries down to twelve. The next leader reported that his church had gone through a similar process and decided on eight essential ministries that had to be present at every campus. The man to my left spoke next and said the leaders of his church felt the correct number was only five. After a vigorous discussion about the difficulty of streamlining any church down to only five areas of ministry, it was my turn. Sheepishly I admitted that the leaders at Seacoast hadn't spent a lot of time studying and discussing the issue, but we replicated just three areas of ministry at each of our campuses: weekend worship, children's ministry, and small groups. I now felt like a naked Calvinist at a Pentecostal tent revival. The other leaders just stared at me, no doubt thinking, "Who are you, and how did you get invited to this meeting?" Dave Browning finally broke the uncomfortable silence: "We only have two ministries when we start a campus. We do weekend worship and small groups. If we don't have anyone to do children's ministry, we just put a table in the corner with some coloring books and crayons until someone volunteers." I knew I had met a man who did not play by the conventional rules.

Dave is the lead pastor of Christ the King Community Church (CTK), which originated in the Skagit Valley area of Washington. Planted by Christ the King in Bellingham, Washington, in 1999, CTK grew to more than 500 attendees in its first year. In 2000 CTK began spreading to other towns in the valley and grew to 750 attendees. Over the next couple of years, the original CTK grew to more than 1,000 weekly attendees and established a dozen different sites across Washington with hundreds of small groups. And in 2004 CTK was recognized as one of the fastest-growing churches in America. Dave, however, had never felt called to pastor a traditional megachurch; his passion was to develop leaders, "pastorpreneurs" as he calls them. He turned his focus from simply growing the original site to developing leaders who would in turn establish CTK centers across Washington as well as across the United States and beyond. By 2008 more than fifty CTK sites were located in eight states and nine countries around the world, with more being added each month.

Dave's view of teamwork and church structure is as revolutionary as his view of how many essential ministries are needed to start a church. I knew when I asked him for input that he would stretch the boundaries beyond our comfort zone.

How can teams (committees, boards) impede the progress of a church?

In our context one of the fears is getting slowed down. A high value is speed. It takes time to get people together, to get all of their questions answered, to wait for the slowest one in the group. So we try to keep teams small and nimble. For instance, our Strategic Leadership Team is four people. Our church council is six people. One of the other dangers I've seen is getting people who are not gifted as leaders in a role where they are telling people who are gifted as leaders how to lead. Basically, we want to be led by leaders, not by bean counters. Over the years the role of our church council has morphed from making decisions to making big decisions to making big business decisions to being a sounding board for me. All of the decision making is handled by key personnel. The board is basically now there to ensure that I am leading CTK in accordance with our stated mission, vision, and values.

How do you balance the wisdom of working with a team with the call to lead?

I'm not sure that we do balance those two things. I would say we are more on the pastorpreneurial side (the call to lead). That is, we don't want group-think. We want pastorpreneurial leadership. We work interdependently, in a "freedom with handrails" construct. The handrails are our beliefs and our brand. But inside of those lines, we tell our leaders to "go for it."

Can you share an incident when you have had to make a tough call that went against the wishes of some members of a leadership group? What was the fallout?

I have had a few hiring decisions that were "gut calls." A couple of my key leaders are guys who flamed out in other contexts and I am giving them a second chance. This is entirely consistent with our mission, vision, and values but has been a cause for concern on our board a couple of times, just because of the prominence of their roles. We haven't seen fallout . . . yet.

What advice would you give to a pastor who is having difficulty leading a board or committee in his church?

Get the governance to a place where you can say yes to opportunities as they arise. Until you do that, you are not going to be leading the church; the church will be leading you. If you can't get the governance to that place, leave and start your own church. I'm only slightly joking here.

How important has teamwork been to the success of your CTK?

We are very people-centric as opposed to program-centric. It took us awhile to figure out that we were not in the church business, or the church growth business, or the multisite business, but in the leader deployment business. We use the word *relationship* more than *teamwork* to describe the way we work together, but it is all about raising up leaders. It is all about community. It is all about ever-expanding circles of relationship.

IQ Test

Take a few minutes to evaluate the team-based aspect of the ministry of your church.

1. How would you describe your church?
    a. Steered by committees
    b. Team led
    c. Pastor led
    d. Other _____

2. How well defined is the mission of individual teams at your church? How can you help further define their mission?

3. Do all of your teams understand the vision of the church? Have you cast vision adequately to the team leaders? Do they buy into the vision? Do they see the connection between their team and the vision?

4. Are your teams led by leaders? Which leaders need to be mentored? Which teams need new leaders?

5. Do the teams feel empowered to operate within their sphere of responsibility? How can you do a better job of empowering them?

IF I MADE ALL TEN MISTAKES, DO I WIN A PRIZE?

A book like this can be intimidating and discouraging as you read about successful men like Chris Hodges, Craig Groeschel, and Perry Noble. "How can they start with $1.27 and a handful of people and build a megachurch while I continue to struggle just to keep my little flock in the fold?" The reality is that God has given some pastors extraordinary gifts and surrounded them with amazing teams and their ministries have been blessed. But God cares just as much about you as he does about the megachurch pastor down the road. The point of the book is not to make you feel like you are stupid if you are not attracting huge crowds every weekend; the point is to provide rungs in the growth ladder for common pastors like you and me.

So as you read through the mistakes, how did you do? Have you made a couple of them? Five or six? Or did you bowl a perfect strike and hit all ten? If so, congratulations — you are a charter member of the stupid pastors club. We're in good company; Moses was a founding member. So what is your next step?

Put Your Hands in the Air and Step Away from the Pulpit

I have a friend who has pastored several churches over his thirty-plus-year career in ministry. In each case he has left the church on life support when he resigned. The ironic thing is that my friend is a great guy; to paraphrase *Saturday Night Live*'s Stuart Smalley, he is good enough, smart enough, and doggonit, people like him. Although he cares deeply about people, is radically committed to Christ, and is an effective communicator, his churches never grow. While he has probably made eight of the ten mistakes in each of the churches he has pastored, I think the challenge is on a more basic level; I don't think God ever intended my friend to pastor a church. It's heartbreaking to see him struggle year after year trying to succeed at something he was never cut out to do.

It's hard to let go of something you feel strongly about in life. I had to make this ugly realization about golf a couple of years ago. I have played golf all my life. When I was five or six years old, my dad would take me to the golf course and let me hit the ball alongside him as he played. By the time I was eight, I had my own set of golf clubs. I played on and off all through high school and college. When I became a pastor, golf was almost a requirement of the job. Over the years I have spent hundreds (thousands?) of dollars on golf equipment, cart rentals, greens fees, and cold hot dogs from snack carts. The challenge during all of this golf is that I have always been remarkably bad. I was so bad I was a danger to my fellow golfers. On more than one occasion, I have hit a ball through a golf cart in which my playing partner was sitting. I have hit the ball and had it land behind where I was standing. Anytime I yell, "Fore!" all the players on the golf course drop to their knees in prayer.

Finally, after a particularly brutal round, I came face-to-face with the reality that I was a terrible golfer and was never going to get any better. I could continue investing large amounts of money in the sport, spending endless hours on the golf course, and terrorizing my fellow golfers, or I could face the cold, hard facts and walk away. I have played one round of golf since that day and haven't looked back. Now I write books and scare fish in my spare time.

Walking away from pastoring is obviously harder than walking away from golf. After being in full-time ministry for twelve years and pastoring at Church on the Lake for two and a half years, I walked away from vocational ministry. Burned out and disillusioned, I spent the next two years trying to repair the damage I had allowed the ministry to cause me and my family, and seeking what God wanted me to do with the rest of my life. This period of my life was a tough time for me. As I mentioned in the introduction, I come from a long line of senior pastors. Having your own church is a rite of passage in my family, and the goal of the ministry, though unspoken, is always to be senior pastor. When I walked away, I felt like a failure. I felt I had let down both my family and God. If senior pastor is the pinnacle of ministry and you step away at thirty-five, what do you do with the rest of your life?

Over the next two years, I found out that I was not wired to be a junior high school teacher, a stay-at-home dad, or a computer software instructor. Working in the secular marketplace provided invaluable experience, but I was miserable. What I did discover was that I could serve God without being a senior pastor. For the first time in my adult life, I was able to volunteer in a church and complain about the sermons like a regular member. That part was a lot of fun. When I got the opportunity to return to a full-time ministry position, however, I knew it was time. I also knew that I might never again pastor my own church, and that was fine with me.

So what about you? Are you where you are supposed to be, or is God releasing you from pastoring so you can become what he created you to be? It may be time to get away for a few days and reassess what God has called you to do with the rest of your life. Seek wise counsel and confirm that you are working God's plan for your life.

A Few Good Mentors

Maybe God has called you to be a senior pastor but you need to get better at it. What is your next step? Start with a mentor. Find a successful pastor in your community and become his buddy. One of the best ways to get a new pastor buddy is to buy him food. Invite your newfound buddy out to lunch and begin to pick his brain. Ask him to visit your church and give you an honest assessment of what he sees. Don't be defensive, but be ready to face the good, the bad, and the ugly. Buy your mentor a copy of this book and go through it together. Ask him to help you assess yourself on each chapter. To keep your mentor engaged, buy him a Starbucks card and make sure to top it off every time you get together.

Open the Eyes of Your Heart

Before you can take your church on a new journey, you have to know where that journey leads. You need a clear direction from God. When Moses led the people into the desert, he didn't know the exact destination, but he knew the goal was the Promised Land. My brother Greg talks about a pivotal time in the history of Seacoast Church when he found that kind of clear direction. The church had been open for about three years and had not seen significant growth. He got away by himself with a Bible and a notebook and asked God to open his eyes to see what the future held for Seacoast. As he sat on a beautiful South Carolina beach, Greg felt clearly that God was calling Seacoast to grow to two thousand attendees by the year 2000. This vision was pretty big since the church had only about three hundred attendees at the time, but Greg felt sure of God's leading. It was from that vision on the beach that Greg led the church for the next decade.

You need to find God's direction for your church. As soon as you can, schedule some significant time away from the day-to-day pressures of pastoring and get alone with God. Take a notebook, your Bible, and an open mind. Begin with this premise: If nothing was impossible, what would God accomplish in our church over the next three years? Then begin to write down answers to these kinds of questions: Who will our church reach whom we are not reaching now? How will our church change over the next year to reach these people? How many people will we impact on a weekend? What ministries will be thriving in our church? How will people's lives be changed through an encounter with Jesus at our church? A great exercise is to turn the answers to these questions into a description of a typical Sunday at your church three years from now. Then begin to pray that God will give you the wisdom to lead your church toward that vision.

Get By with a Little Help from Your Friends

Now that you have a mentor and a vision, it's time to galvanize your leadership team. Select a few leaders who you think would be committed to positive change in the church and invite them on the journey with you. Begin by being honest about your shortcomings and the ways you plan to change. Share with them the vision God has given you for the future, and tell them you want to start the journey by changing how you lead the church. You might even consider using this book as a way to open the discussion and begin the process. At the end of each chapter, get together and discuss applications for your church. (If you can't think of any application from a particular chapter, tear it out of the book and make paper airplanes. It will be a great team-building exercise.)

Form a Partnership

Alex Barefoot started Summit Christian Community Church in Columbia, South Carolina, in 1998 with a vision of reaching the city for Jesus, but by 2002 he was worn out. The church had quickly grown to 130 people each weekend, but then growth stalled. Alex tried everything he knew, but nothing changed. Finally, he came to Seacoast and asked if we would be interested in adopting Summit as one of our campuses. It was an amazingly courageous act for Alex because he was laying down his leadership as well as stepping away from preaching every weekend. The results, however, have been amazing. The church grew quickly from 130 to well over 300, and people's lives began to change. Eventually Alex's congregation launched another Seacoast campus in the Columbia area, and now more than one thousand people attend the two campuses each weekend. The vision God gave Alex is being accomplished through his willingness to partner with another church.

Could God be calling you to partner with another ministry? Across the country churches are connecting through mergers, adoptions, and partnerships and are making a huge impact for the kingdom. Is there a healthy church in your community that would be willing to come alongside your church? Are you ready to lay down your preconceived notions of what it means to pastor and to become part of a dynamic team that can make a huge impact on your city?

If we continue to do church the way we have always done church, we will never reach our world in the way we have been called. Statistics show that in spite of the megachurch movement of the last twenty years, more and more Americans are walking away from church and away from a relationship with Jesus. Through strategic partnerships in which churches stop competing and start cooperating, we might be able to reverse that trend.

The Bottom Line

Kathy was about five minutes late on her first visit to Church on the Lake. It was the Sunday before Thanksgiving, and the church was almost full. Everyone watched as she walked down the center aisle to find a seat. By her dress and her makeup, we could tell Kathy was not from Huffman; ladies who looked like Kathy didn't just show up in little country churches without a story. After service Kathy began to tell me hers.

Kathy had just arrived with her three daughters from Hollywood, California. Her life was out of control and unraveling fast. Her husband, whom she had left behind in LA, was addicted to alcohol and cocaine. Her fourteen-year-old daughter until recently had been living on the streets. Out of options and out of hope, Kathy decided to move to Huffman, a town she had visited once several years before. When I asked why she chose Huffman, she said, "Because it's the furthest place from Hollywood I could imagine." She had grown up

Catholic but had left the church a long time ago. In a strange place, desperate for a fresh start, she wandered into our church that morning searching for God.

Over the next several months, Kathy continued to attend every Sunday morning, eventually committing her life to Christ. Our people embraced Kathy and her daughters like their own family, loving them unconditionally. Just after Christmas Kathy's husband, Bernie, came out from California. He began to attend church with Kathy and soon committed his life to Christ as well. For the first time in many years, Bernie stayed clean and sober for a week, then for a month, and then for a whole year. On his first Christmas in Texas, Bernie stood and told his new church family that on Christmas morning the year before, he stood on a corner in Beverly Hills, alone and desperate, trying to score one more bag of cocaine. Tears flowed freely that morning as Bernie told us how since that day he had formed a new relationship with Jesus, been set free from addiction, and been reunited with his family. We rode with Kathy and Bernie through many ups and downs over the next months and years, but their commitment to Christ never wavered. Their lives and the lives of their daughters were completely changed that Sunday morning when Kathy wandered into our little country church in Huffman.

Church on the Lake never grew beyond about one hundred people. I made every mistake in this book and several more besides in my time as their pastor, but I know I was in God's will when I pastored that church because of Bernie and Kathy and others with different stories but similar outcomes. We didn't grow a megachurch, or even much of a microchurch, but we reached people with the gospel of Christ and saw lives changed for eternity.

And that is why you are pastoring where you are. You are there for the Bernies and the Kathys in your community. You are there to see people break away from the kingdom of darkness and enter the kingdom of light. You are there to see people grow in their faith, transform their community, and catch a vision to change their world. You have made mistakes and will make more in the future. My hope is that this book will help you avoid some of the mistakes I have made. But at the end of the day, don't ever forget that you are anointed "to preach good news to the poor ... to bind up the brokenhearted ... to proclaim freedom for the captives and release from darkness for the prisoners" (Isa. 61:1). The local church is the hope of the world, and as pastors, we are the hope of the local church. So let's get a fresh vision from God, pour ourselves into our families, empower our teams to lead, and get busy changing our world.

ACKNOWLEDGMENTS

The task of writing a book and getting it published is impossible without a team. I want to acknowledge my team:

- My Savior and friend, Jesus Christ, who shows his sense of humor by using someone as goofy as me to spread the good news.

- My beautiful wife, Sherry, and incredible kids, Mike and Brittainy, who have supported me through many, many stupid mistakes.

- My brother Greg and the leadership of Seacoast Church for teaching me how to pastor and giving me the space to write about it.

- Greg Ligon, Dave Travis, Gayle Carpenter, Tom Wilson, and the rest of the team at Leadership Network who helped me connect with outstanding pastors all over the world.

- Mark Sweeney, who told me the idea for this book just might work and then patiently waited for me to turn it into something.

- Mark Batterson, Dave Browning, Scott Chapman, Dave Ferguson, Craig Groeschel, Ron Hamilton, Chris Hodges, Perry Noble, Dino Rizzo, and Greg Surratt for their generous contributions and insight. Also Chris Surratt, Dave Travis, Warren Bird, and Jack Hoey for their insight and suggestions.

- Paul Engle and the team at Zondervan for giving a stupid pastor a chance.